Expanding Tertiary Education for Well-Paid Jobs

WORLD BANK STUDY

Expanding Tertiary Education for Well-Paid Jobs

Competitiveness and Shared Prosperity in Kenya

Andreas Blom, Reehana Raza, Crispus Kiamba,
Himdat Bayusuf, and Mariam Adil

© 2016 International Bank for Reconstruction and Development / The World Bank
1818 H Street NW, Washington, DC 20433
Telephone: 202-473-1000; Internet: www.worldbank.org

Some rights reserved

1 2 3 4   19 18 17 16

World Bank Studies are published to communicate the results of the Bank's work to the development community with the least possible delay. The manuscript of this paper therefore has not been prepared in accordance with the procedures appropriate to formally edited texts.

This work is a product of the staff of The World Bank with external contributions. The findings, interpretations, and conclusions expressed in this work do not necessarily reflect the views of The World Bank, its Board of Executive Directors, or the governments they represent. The World Bank does not guarantee the accuracy of the data included in this work. The boundaries, colors, denominations, and other information shown on any map in this work do not imply any judgment on the part of The World Bank concerning the legal status of any territory or the endorsement or acceptance of such boundaries.

Nothing herein shall constitute or be considered to be a limitation upon or waiver of the privileges and immunities of The World Bank, all of which are specifically reserved.

Rights and Permissions

This work is available under the Creative Commons Attribution 3.0 IGO license (CC BY 3.0 IGO) http://creativecommons.org/licenses/by/3.0/igo. Under the Creative Commons Attribution license, you are free to copy, distribute, transmit, and adapt this work, including for commercial purposes, under the following conditions:

Attribution—Please cite the work as follows: Blom, Andreas, Reehana Raza, Crispus Kiamba, Himdat Bayusuf, and Mariam Adil. 2016. *Expanding Tertiary Education for Well-Paid Jobs: Competitiveness and Shared Prosperity in Kenya.* World Bank Studies. Washington, DC: World Bank. doi:10.1596/978-1-4648-0848-7. License: Creative Commons Attribution CC BY 3.0 IGO

Translations—If you create a translation of this work, please add the following disclaimer along with the attribution: *This translation was not created by The World Bank and should not be considered an official World Bank translation. The World Bank shall not be liable for any content or error in this translation.*

Adaptations—If you create an adaptation of this work, please add the following disclaimer along with the attribution: *This is an adaptation of an original work by The World Bank. Views and opinions expressed in the adaptation are the sole responsibility of the author or authors of the adaptation and are not endorsed by The World Bank.*

Third-party content—The World Bank does not necessarily own each component of the content contained within the work. The World Bank therefore does not warrant that the use of any third-party-owned individual component or part contained in the work will not infringe on the rights of those third parties. The risk of claims resulting from such infringement rests solely with you. If you wish to reuse a component of the work, it is your responsibility to determine whether permission is needed for that reuse and to obtain permission from the copyright owner. Examples of components can include, but are not limited to, tables, figures, or images.

All queries on rights and licenses should be addressed to the Publishing and Knowledge Division, The World Bank, 1818 H Street NW, Washington, DC 20433, USA; fax: 202-522-2625; e-mail: pubrights @worldbank.org.

ISBN (paper): 978-1-4648-0848-7
ISBN (electronic): 978-1-4648-0849-4
DOI: 10.1596/978-1-4648-0848-7

Cover design: Debra Naylor, Naylor Design, Inc.

Library of Congress Cataloging-in-Publication Data
Names: Blom, Andreas, author. | Raza, Reehana, author. | Kiamba, Crispus, author.
Title: Expanding tertiary education for well-paid jobs : competitiveness and shared prosperity in Kenya/Andreas Blom, Reehana Raza, Crispus Kiamba.
Description: Washington, D.C. : World Bank, [2016]
Identifiers: LCCN 2016009424 | ISBN 9781464808487
Subjects: LCSH: Education, Higher—Economic aspects—Kenya. | Universities and colleges—Kenya—Admission. | College graduates—Employment—Kenya. | Educational equalization—Kenya.
Classification: LCC LC67.68.K4 B56 2016 | DDC 338.4/3378096762—dc23
LC record available at http://lccn.loc.gov/2016009424

Contents

Acknowledgments		*ix*
About the Authors		*xi*
Abbreviations		*xv*

Chapter 1	**Executive Summary**	1
	Introduction	1
	Rationale for the Three Focus Areas	2
	The Key Numbers: A Tertiary Education System under Pressure	5
	Key Findings: Quality and Relevance	5
	Key Findings: Student Financing	7
	Key Findings: Regulatory Oversight and Management of the Higher Education Sector	9
	Policy Options	11
	Improving Governance through the Process of Expansion	13
	Notes	14
	References	14

Chapter 2	**Quality and Relevance**	17
	Objective	17
	Introduction	17
	The Youth Bulge and the Expected Tsunami of Secondary Educated Graduates	19
	Limited Relevance of Programs	21
	Policy Recommendations	23
	Expansion without Quality	25
	Policy Recommendations	28
	Inequitable Expansion	29
	Policy Recommendations	31
	Conclusion	32
	Notes	33
	References	34

Chapter 3	Student Loans: A Tool for Equitable Expansion	37
	Introduction	37
	Why Student Loans?	40
	Student Loans in Kenya	43
	Challenge 1: Meeting Demand for Loans	44
	Challenge 2: Targeting	47
	Challenge 3: Weak Recovery Mechanisms	51
	Notes	53
	References	53
Chapter 4	Governance of Post-Secondary Education in Kenya	55
	Introduction	55
	The National Vision: The Context of Reforms in Higher Education	56
	The Higher Education Legal and Institutional Framework	57
	The Governance and Management of Kenyan Higher Education	64
	Conclusion: Challenges, Opportunities, and Recommendations	73
	Notes	75
	References	75

Boxes

3.1	HELB Loans at a Glance	43
3.2	Chilean Loan Scheme—A Focus on Equity	50
4.1	Status of Universities in Kenya, 2014	59

Figures

2.1	Enrollment in Primary and Secondary Education in Kenya, 2001–13	20
2.2	Changes in Kenyan Post-Secondary Enrollment: TVET and Universities	22
2.3	Percentage of Firms in Kenya Identifying an Inadequately Educated Workforce as a Major Constraint	26
2.4	Average Loans per Income Group	31
3.1	Projections for Rise in Number of Students Transitioning from Secondary to Post-Secondary Education	39
3.2	Rationale for Student Loans	41
3.3	Average Loans, by Income Group	48
3.4	Comparison of Household Incomes of Loan Applicants and Recipients to Average Households in Kenya	49

Tables

2.1	Undergraduate Enrollment in Science-Related Disciplines as a Proportion of Total Undergraduate Enrollment in Kenyan Universities	23
3.1	Projections for HELB Funding Needs	45
3.2	Average Household Income of Loan Applicants and Recipients in Comparison with GDP per Capita	47
3.3	HELB Loan Recovery Status	51
3.4	Loan Book as of June 30, 2014	51
4.1	Student Enrollment in Public and Private Universities	58

Acknowledgments

These policy notes were authored by a World Bank team comprising Reehana Raza (senior human development economist), Himdat Bayusuf (education specialist), Mariam Adil (consultant), Crispus Kiamba (consultant), and Andreas Blom (team lead). The team is grateful to Kenyan policy makers and their important collaboration with the government agencies. The team extends its gratitude to the Norwegian government for funding for World Bank staff time through its Africa Post-Basic Trust Fund. All errors and omissions are those of the authors.

About the Authors

Andreas Blom is a lead economist in the World Bank's Education Global Practice and focuses on Africa. He supports management in implementing strategies to improve the quality of the World Bank's education portfolio in Africa and serves as a resource person for tertiary education in the region, supporting tertiary education teams and projects in Africa. He is also the task team leader of the Africa Centers of Excellence project. He specializes in the economic policy analysis of human capital and creation of knowledge, and their efficient use in society. Andreas has previously worked with the government of India to improve the quality of, access to, and financing of its higher education system. Furthermore, he has worked with the government of Pakistan to provide more and better training opportunities to Pakistani youths. He started his career in the World Bank in the Latin America and the Caribbean region, where he worked for seven years on higher education, training, labor markets, and public spending. He has published several global and regional studies on the financing of higher education, student loans, labor markets, quality of education, and science, technology, and innovation. Andreas holds a master's degree in development economics from the University of Aarhus, Denmark.

Reehana Raza is a senior economist in the World Bank's Education Global Practice, where she focuses on skills development in eastern and southern Africa. She also provides cross-support to South Asia in the areas of skills and social protection. Before joining the World Bank, Reehana set up and led the Institute of Development and Economic Alternatives (IDEAS), a new economic think tank in Pakistan, financed by the Open Society Foundations. IDEAS focused on targeting economic issues that strengthen economic pluralism in Pakistan. She ran the institute while teaching at Lahore University of Management Sciences, where she served as an assistant professor of economics. Her areas of teaching and research related to the economics of education, development economics, institutional economics, and East Asian growth. Reehana has worked and consulted for the Asian Development Bank, World Bank, United Nations Development Programme, U.S. Agency for International Development, U.K. Department for International Development (DFID), and other bilateral agencies. She has diverse regional experience spanning South Asia, Sub-Saharan Africa, the Far East, and Central Asia. Reehana is a former Commonwealth Scholarship winner and holds a BA in international relations from Mount Holyoke College as well as an MPhil in development economics and a PhD in economics from the University of Cambridge.

Crispus Kiamba holds a BA in land economics from the University of Nairobi; an MSc from the University of Reading; a PhD from the University of Cambridge; and an executive certificate in science, technology, and innovation from Harvard University. He has served as permanent secretary in the government of Kenya in both the Ministry of Higher Education, Science and Technology and the Ministry of Science and Technology; as a member of Kenya's National Economic and Social Council and Vision 2030 Implementation Board; as secretary and chief executive officer of the Commission for Higher Education; and as vice-chancellor of the University of Nairobi. Professor Kiamba has served on many boards, including the International Science, Technology and Innovation Centre for South-South Cooperation; Centre for Science and Technology of Non-Aligned and Other Developing Countries; Commonwealth Scholarship and Fellowship Plan Endowment Fund; Joint Expert Group for the 8th Africa–EU Strategic Partnership for Science, Information Society and Space; Steering Committee of the African Ministerial Committee of Science and Technology; Inter-Universities Council of East Africa; African Institute for Capacity Development; and Kenya Education Network. Professor Kiamba has also served as an evaluator on the World Bank African Higher Education Centres of Excellence project and continues to serve in many other appointments, including on the Consultative Advisory Group of the World Bank–affiliated Partnership for Skills in Applied Sciences, Engineering and Technology; on the Evaluation Review Panel of the Advancing Sub-Saharan Africa–European Union Cooperation in Research and Innovation for Global Challenges (CAAST-Net Plus) Project; as chairman of the Commonwealth Scholarship and Fellowship Fund Task Force; and as a consultant to the U.K.'s DFID Development Research Uptake in Sub-Saharan Africa Programme.

Himdat Bayusuf is a proactive development practitioner with a demonstrated record of performance and outstanding project management, analytical, and client relationship skills. Her experience includes eight years of direct project management, including preparation, implementation, and supervision of World Bank–funded projects in the Africa, Middle East and North Africa, and East Asia regions. Himdat first joined the World Bank Middle East and North Africa team in 2009 as a consultant, supporting project preparation, implementation, and supervision of the Yemen education portfolio, including the conditional cash transfer project. Most recently, she served on the West and Central Africa Education team, where she was a key contributor in the preparation and implementation of the Africa Centers of Excellence project. Himdat has also demonstrated strong analytical skills as the primary author of the Gambia Third Education Implementation Completion Report, and provided data for various education policy notes. Himdat is currently an education economist in the

East Asia and Pacific region, where she is supporting the Philippines Education team on a public expenditure tracking survey for quality service delivery and a $300 million Basic Education Learning and Accountability project. Before joining the World Bank, Himdat worked in the London financial sector as a research analyst, and before that at Transparency International's London office. Himdat holds a BSc in economics from Cardiff University and an MSc in development economics from the London School of Economics.

Mariam Adil is an operations analyst at the World Bank and the founder of a social venture called GRID—Gaming Revolution for International Development. She has five years of human development experience across Africa and South Asia and specializes in offering technical and advisory assistance for education projects. She specializes in conducting rigorous data analysis to provide empirical-based policy and in leveraging technology innovations to address behavioral and information constraints in development projects. Mariam's venture GRID was recognized as an "exemplary approach" for social change by former President Bill Clinton at the 2015 Clinton Global Initiative University Meeting. Mariam holds two master's degrees, an MA in international development studies from The George Washington University and an MSc in economics from Lahore University of Management Sciences. She is the recipient of the 2015 Andrew E. Rice Award for Leadership & Innovation by the Society of International Development.

Abbreviations

CAE	Crédito con Aval del Estado, Programa de
CHE	Commission for Higher Education
CUE	Commission for University Education
HELB	Higher Education Loan Board
HEMIS	Higher Education Management Information System
GER	gross enrollment ratio
GoK	government of Kenya
JAB	Joint Admissions Board
KAIST	Kenyan Advanced Institute for Science and Technology
KCSE	Kenya Certificate of Secondary Education
KRA	Kenya Revenue Authority
KSh	Kenyan shilling
KUCCPS	Kenya University and College Central Placement Services
LIA	letter of interim authority
LMIS	labor market information system
MoEST	Ministry of Education, Science, and Technology
MTI	means testing instrument
NBTE	National Board for Technical Education
NCCE	National Commission for Colleges of Education
NHIF	National Hospital Insurance Fund
NQF	National Qualifications Framework
NSSF	National Social Security Fund
NUC	National Universities Commission
NVQ	National Vocational Qualification
QA	quality assurance
SSA	Sub-Saharan Africa
STEM	science, technology, engineering, and mathematics

STR	student teacher ratio
TEI	tertiary education institution
TVET	technical and vocational education and training
TVETA	Technical and Vocational Education and Training Authority
USAID	United States Agency for International Development

CHAPTER 1

Executive Summary

Introduction

In order to realize the ideals of the 2010 Constitution and the government of Kenya's 2030 Vision, which aims to transform the country into a "newly industrializing, middle income, globally competitive and prosperous country," it will be imperative for Kenya to expand equitable access to quality tertiary education in alignment with the economic and developmental needs of the country. Expanding access to quality tertiary education will critically contribute to a holistic strategy to overcome several of the country's primary challenges:

The delivery of quality education, including tertiary education, will build the skills base of youth, enhancing their capacity to accrue higher earnings, contribute to improved national productivity, and lead healthy and sustainable livelihoods. At present, 26 million Kenyans—more than half of the country's population—is under the age of 25. By 2030 two thirds of Kenyans are projected to fall into the under 25 cohort (World Bank 2014a).

It will be critical for Kenya to expand tertiary education in order to reap the full developmental benefits associated with the dramatic expansion of primary and secondary education achieved since the 1990s. The number of students sitting the Kenya Certificate of Secondary Education (KCSE) exam, necessary for university admission, is expected to almost double from 430,000 in 2012 (see figure 2.1) to 836,000 by 2016. The failure to accommodate an expanded cohort of qualified secondary education graduates into tertiary education would represent a significant economic loss, possibly generate additional social tensions and further exacerbate existing levels of inequality of opportunity. The expansion of the Kenyan tertiary education sector will, as a consequence, play a prominent role in enhancing shared prosperity in Kenya.

The improved supply of quality tertiary graduates, with skills aligned to the needs of the private sector, will strengthen the competitiveness of Kenyan companies. In 2013, 29 percent of firms sampled by the World Bank's Enterprise Survey for Kenya reported an "inadequately educated workforce" as a major obstacle to growth. A poorly educated workforce was the most frequently reported obstacle to growth cited by firms, surpassing challenges relating to access to access to energy and suboptimal infrastructure (see figure 2.2; World Bank 2013b).

Expanding access to quality tertiary education will improve individual prosperity and contribute to poverty reduction. Graduates holding a tertiary qualification earn substantially more than workers with lower levels of education. While the most recent survey of returns to education in Kenya is a decade old, available evidence suggests that returns to tertiary education in Kenya are 22 percent, substantially above the global average of 15 percent (Montenegro and Patrinos 2014).[1]

The realization of Kenya's Vision 2030 will only be possible through increased absorption and adoption of new technologies. Toward this end, accelerating Kenya's development will require a much stronger pipeline to supply scientists and engineers to the labor market, with the requisite problem-solving skills, entrepreneurial spirit and capacity to drive innovation.

While the performance of Kenya's tertiary education sector compares favorably with many other African countries, it faces significant challenges. With total enrollment of 330,000 students in 2013, the Kenyan tertiary education sector is the fourth largest in sub-Sahara Africa (SSA), with many strong and established universities, and benefits from a forward looking legal and policy framework. However, the system is under severe pressure and faces a number of critical challenges. The number of Kenyan universities more than doubled to 66 institutions between 2010 and 2014, while the number of students entering institutions of higher learning tripled between 2008 and 2013. Rates of growth are expected to be sustained in the ensuing five years. At present, the costs of self-sponsored higher education are prohibitive for most middle and low income Kenyans. The sustained expansion of the higher education sector has the potential to play an important role in the country's development, but only if students accrue quality skills, relevant to the needs of the labor market and if graduate output is representative of a broad cross-section of Kenyan socioeconomic groups.

The analysis contained in this report, and the accompanying and policy options, are intended to support the government of Kenya (GoK), leaders of the tertiary education sector, and other stakeholders in the system, manage the pressures associated with significantly increased demand for higher education, and inform decision-making as the country moves to expand access to quality tertiary education. The report is structured in the following manner: It commences with a discussion of the motivation for the report, and its three focus areas: quality and relevance; governance, and student financing. Thereafter the report reviews findings for each focus area in the form of three policy notes, each of which concludes with a set of policy recommendations.

Rationale for the Three Focus Areas

Three key challenges that will need to be confronted to ensure the success of expansionary goals include the need to: improve the quality and relevance of education delivered to improve the employment prospects of graduates; improve institutional and sector-wide governance to promote efficiency; and the need to scale-up and improve systems to support student finance. The effective transfer of relevant skills and knowledge to graduates through tertiary education depends upon a series of factors spanning, *inter alia*, the quality of basic education delivered, faculty characteristics, including academic and pedagogical skills and motivation, and institutional autonomy and financing. Due to resource limitations, this study has prioritized the analysis of three broad issues deemed crucial for the development of Kenya's tertiary education: (a) policies and investments to safeguard and improve the quality and relevance of teaching and learning; (b) policies and investments to improve the governance of sector and institutions, the promotion of transparency, and the strengthening of institutional leadership; and (c) the need to scale-up and improve student financing to assist students and families to cover costs associated with tertiary education. The decision to focus on these three areas is informed by a host of international case studies from countries that have successfully, and unsuccessfully, managed processes to expand access to tertiary education. Such examples include, but are not limited to, Chile, China, Colombia, India, Mexico, Tunisia, and Vietnam. Specific motivation for a close focus on these challenges includes the following rationale:

- **The quality and relevance of higher education programs delivered are important determinants informing the relative employability of tertiary graduates.** Kenyan companies face severe difficulties in recruiting workers with an appropriate mix of applicable skills and knowledge. Simply tripling the capacity of existing tertiary educational programming (and the number of institutions) is likely to lead to situations where graduates cannot find suitable employment, are underemployed and their education skills are not properly utilized for the economy's benefit. The introduction of new programs must be linked to new labor market opportunities and shifting demand in the private sector. New regional universities should not seek to simply replicate the programming of established and prestigious universities, but should instead build programs that cater to region-specific labor market demand and localized developmental priorities. Investment to ensure that sufficiently qualified faculty staff components keep pace with the expansion of student enrollment will be critical for maintaining and promoting quality. Moreover, the government and institutions must ensure that sufficiently rigorous policies, complemented by sufficient capacity to implement these policies, are in place to promote quality assurance through internal institutional, and external independent quality assurance evaluations.

- **Student financing in support of equitable expansion:** An efficient, sufficiently scaled, well-functioning, and effectively endowed system to support student aid will be critical if Kenya is to achieve its expansionary goals for tertiary education in a financially sustainable manner, while concurrently ensuring the promotion of equity and quality. The ongoing expansion of the sector is in part informed by the decision by government to allow private cost sharing of tertiary education. A significant expansion of the public resource envelope in support of post-secondary education is not fiscally possible given the magnitude of the expansionary pressure being exerted on the sector; the high costs associated with delivering quality tertiary education; the many competing priorities for public expenditure; and limited public monies available for education. The relatively high private returns associated with tertiary education can be used to justify further contributions on the part of beneficiaries with the ability to pay for higher education. However, the uniform application of a cost sharing policy, without contingent interventions to ensure access to finance on the part of relatively needy students, risks excluding many qualified middle and low-income students without the means to cover the substantial costs associated with self-sponsored tertiary education, with substantial developmental and social costs for the country. As a consequence there is a strong case for publicly financed student loans targeted to those who cannot afford the costs associated with post-secondary education. Effectively targeted and sustainable student financing will be critical for ensuring equality of opportunity in accessing tertiary education in Kenya. Of course, even the type of scheme, which could be designed in a fiscally prudent manner, would have to be weighed against other competing public expenditure priorities.

- **Transparent and professional governance of the tertiary education system.** Kenya's tertiary education system is becoming more complex due to the proliferation of public and private institutions, and a multitude of new social, economic and institutional pressures. Kenya is in the process of implementing various reforms affecting the governance of tertiary education in response to the passing of the 2010 Constitution, the government's Vision 2030, and the Universities Act of 2012, as well as in response to shifting demand in the economy. In this context the sector and institutions will require a strong structure to ensure effective governance, and successful management of the tertiary education system as it evolves. Resolving questions relating to who should manage the system, the role of government and the appropriate roles of agencies and institutions will be critical in this regard. At the institutional level, the balancing of autonomy with mechanisms for holding institutions accountable for the use of public resources, as well as the need to promote quality assurance, are critical challenges need to be addressed in determining the most appropriate system of governance for the Kenyan system.

A lack of information and data has been a critical constraint limiting the analysis contained in this study. No reliable nation-wide information is routinely collected on the sector, aside from statistics relating to enrollment and the number of institutions, and information collected by institutions is uneven in quality and utility. The absence of timely and reliable data inhibits analysis, the development of standards relating to institutional performance and benchmarking, undermines the ability to analyze costs incurred by students and families, and erodes the potential for the development of evidence-based debates and policies.

The Key Numbers: A Tertiary Education System under Pressure

Overall, the policy notes contained in this report, and the supporting analyses, paint a picture of a tertiary education system, that has some positive aspects—not least that it is expanding to meet growing demand—but is under considerable pressure. There is a substantial risk that in the future, students enrolling in the system will suffer with regard to the quality of learning they receive, with negative implications for their employability and the developmental trajectory of the country. There is a contingent risk that the high costs associated with tertiary education in Kenya will continue to function as a significant barrier to entry for students from poor families, restricting access to the sector to students from comparatively affluent socio-economic strata. The GoK's current policies, and its program for investment in the sector, recognize these challenges; but these interventions are likely to be insufficient to ensure that the capacity of post-secondary faculty is developed to keep pace with expanded enrollment, ensure sufficient quality assurance, promote and inculcate effective leadership for the sector, and that a sufficiently capacitated and resilient student financing system to facilitate access on an equitable basis.

Key Findings: Quality and Relevance

To support its desired developmental trajectory, the Kenyan post-secondary system must balance the academic and professional qualifications of graduates with the needs of the economy and national priorities, with particular attention paid to graduate output in the disciplines of science, technology, engineering and math (STEM). In the period spanning 2005 to 2010, the majority of undergraduate students enrolled in Kenyan universities were enrolled in nonscience-related courses.[2] In 2005, enrollment in nonscience related programs represented 80 percent of total enrollment, declining slightly to 78 percent in 2010, a trend that is mirrored in other Sub-Saharan African countries. There has been a small, but increasing, trend in enrollment in engineering, medicine and agriculture related courses in the period under review, although this will be insufficient to meet the needs of the economy. Evidence suggests that graduates from technical fields generally find employment more easily compared to graduates from the social sciences. The large proportion of Kenyan enrollment concentrated in nonscience-related fields could contribute to a situation in which many graduates are un- or underemployed following the completion of their studies. The experience of Tunisia demonstrates a prescient example wherein disproportionate enrollment in the social sciences and humanities programs contributed to high levels of youth un- and underemployment, with negative implications for social stability. Multiple factors contribute to low enrollment in STEM related programming in Kenya: Due to the need to invest in expensive equipment and the nature of laboratory-based education, costs associated with delivering STEM related programs are higher than those associated with delivering courses in the social sciences and humanities. As a consequence, when policymakers and institutions are confronted with significant pressure to expand admissions, there has been a tendency to push more students towards the humanities and social sciences. An additional contributing factor is a chronic shortage of sufficiently qualified faculty with the capacity to teach STEM related programs of sufficient quality to meet recognized standards (less than 20 percent of faculty in these disciplines hold a PhD). Only 29 percent of sub-Saharan Africa research output is concentrated in STEM related fields, compared to 70 percent in Malaysia and Vietnam. A third factor relates to the small number of private tertiary institutions that have invested in STEM disciplines, a consequence of the high costs associated with investments in laboratories. A final factor undermining the admission of students to STEM disciplines relates to generally low demand on the part of aspirant tertiary students for STEM programs, in part a consequence of the relatively low number of students transitioning from secondary education with the skills and qualifications required for enrollment in STEM programs.

Faculty staff components and the qualifications of faculty have not kept pace with expanded post-secondary enrollment, undermining the quality of education delivered. While student numbers have more than doubled between 2008 and 2013, Nganga has estimated that the number of faculty working in institutions increased by only 28.6 percent, from 7,000 to 9,000 over the same period (Nganga 2013). Anecdotally it is not uncommon for faculty to work in eight to ten institutions at a time. . Data provided by the Commission for University Education (CUE) with regard to student-teacher ratios (STR) in the 22 chartered institutions, demonstrates an average STR of 36:1 in the Kenyan higher education sector, but with significant variance. Within the system, STRs range from a low of 14:1 at the Technical University of Kenya and 17:1 at the South Eastern University of Kenya, to a high of high 64:1 at Kenyatta University, 63:1 at Laikipia University and 60:1 at Kisii University. In Kenya, 290 students graduated with doctoral degrees in 2013, while total enrollment in higher education expanded by 80,000. Even if one assumes full employment for all new PhD graduates within the university system, the ratio of new qualified faculty to new students was 1:275. Kenya will need to accelerate PhD graduate output to at least 1,000 per annum if the quality teaching in the tertiary education sector is to be safeguarded.

External quality assurance is now mandatory for all Kenyan higher education institutions and programs of study; however the CUE will require significant capacity enhancement if it is to effectively deliver on its expanded mandate. A key element of ensuring quality in any tertiary education system is the presence of a robust and effective quality assurance system. Previously the Commission for Higher Education (CHE) only accredited institutions and programs at private universities. Under the provisions of the new University Act (2012), CUE—which has replaced CHE—is now mandated to undertake quality assurance for the university sector as a whole. The fact that all institutions and programs will now be subject to scrutiny through external quality assurance will benefit students. However, CUE now faces the additional challenge of accrediting the public subsector, inclusive of 23 public constituent colleges, as well as new private universities that have received a Letter of Interim Authority (LIA). Moreover, CUE's expanded mandate includes responsibility for the accreditation of all programs delivered at universities; the scale of this particular challenge is underlined by the fact that the University of Nairobi alone delivers 371 programs.

Key Findings: Student Financing

The Higher Education Loans Board (HELB) in Kenya is mandated with the task of providing student loans and grants to Kenyans enrolled in public and private universities, in addition to students enrolled in TVET institutions in Kenya and the rest of East Africa.

The high price of tertiary education seems to be a key constraint limiting the enrollment of low and middle-income students. Approximately, seven in ten students enrolled in Kenyan higher education institutions pay full fees (four in ten students are fee paying students in private institutions, and of the remainder, half attend public institutions as self-sponsored, full fee paying students). The system of fee-based education has played a role in the expansion of public and the private university education, and has allowed universities to direct some funds towards supporting quality related inputs. However, the levying of fees acts as a barrier to entry for students who cannot afford to pay fees, as well as for those who struggle to access finance. Anecdotal evidence suggests that fees are a serious obstacle for students from low and middle income families.

No large scale student loan scheme in Kenya will be effective without public support. To date the small loans schemes exclusively administered in private institutions in Kenya have failed to reach scale and do not effectively address equity concerns. Global evidence supports the view that large scale access to student loans premised on academic performance, regardless of socioeconomic background, must be publicly supported due to the prevalence of substantial market failures relating to high social returns, information asymmetries, and uncertainties that undermine private student loan schemes. Loans in support of education differ from commercial loans, such as mortgages and auto loans, due to the fact that investments in education constitute large sunk costs which cannot be re-possessed and sold to defray costs associated with loan delinquency. As a result commercial lenders rarely provide market-based long-term loans to support the costs of education. Consequently, a well-managed student loan program would typically merit and require substantial public subsidy, although such a scheme must compete against other spending priorities and be fiscally prudent.

HELB is the largest student loan program in East Africa, and demonstrates substantially more institutional capacity than many African student loan agencies. HELB has accrued significant experience from the commercial sector, is in the process of implementing a strategic plan, and has several effective loan recovery strategies in place. However, there is substantial room for improvement.

There is a large financing gap for student loans, and it is likely to grow larger in the forecast period. In 2012/2013, HELB disbursed loans to 118,426 students to a value of KSh 5.0 billion (US$45.4 million), against total university enrollment of 380,000, representing coverage of 31.2 percent. In any given year HELB is primarily financed through loan recovery and direct public funding. Given the rapid growth in admissions, HELB is experiencing a significant increase in demand for loans. Poor levels of public funding, suboptimal loan recovery, poor targeting, and expectations on the part of students with regard to access to finance, have cumulatively contributed to delays in the review of loan applications and loan disbursement, leading to student unrest in 2014. According to the projections contained in this report, the number of loan applications will grow by a magnitude of 30,000–35,000 new applicants each year between 2014 and 2022, resulting in a context in which projected demand for loans and concurrent funding requirements will, at a minimum, triple within seven years.

Current practices for administering student loans could be more effective in targeting students with the most pronounced financing needs. Two primary interventions should be prioritized to improve targeting mechanisms: (a) HELB must establish systems to assess the veracity of financial information provided by loan applicants. Data suggest that loan applicants underreport income to boost their chances of acquiring loans. At present HELB has no credible verification mechanism for assessing the accuracy of reported family income and financial means; (b) Further, the loans distributed by HELB do not vary significantly by household income, and disbursement mechanisms need to be improved to further prioritize financial support to low income students. At present students evaluated by HELB as bring in the lowest income group, receive an average loan of US$504, compared to students in the highest income group who receive US$436. As a consequence, the means testing mechanism allocates a 20 percent differential in the amount disbursed to the "richest" and "poorest" beneficiaries, despite a 700 percent differential between the lowest and highest categories of household income measured by the instrument.

The scale and financial sustainability of HELB can be improved through greater risk-sharing and improved loan recovery. The financial sustainability of any given student loan scheme depends on the cost of procuring funds (primarily a measure of the level of direct public funding for the scheme), the subsidy provided for the loan (interest rate subsidy), default rates, and administrative costs. Ensuring the financial sustainability of HELB is a prerequisite for advancing equity in tertiary education in Kenya. While accurate comparative information is unavailable, the financial sustainability of HELB appears to be significantly better relative to the average student loan program in Africa, and HELB continues to work to improve sustainability in innovative ways. Notwithstanding these positive characteristics, HELB would benefit from implementation of the following strategies to improve recovery: (a) Greater risk-sharing with beneficiary institutions and families. Private institutions accrue substantial benefits from financial resources derived from HELB supported students, but these institutions do not contribute to the scheme. Moreover, the families of students reduce their out-of-pocket expenditure through access to student loans and gain considerably through access to tertiary education without having to raise collateral or risk their credit ratings; (b) contact with students/borrowers, their families, and the education institutions seemingly could be more frequent; (c) Available evidence suggests that the default characteristics of beneficiaries are insufficiently analyzed to identify key risk factors informing default and delinquency. Improved data collection and analysis would enable HELB and institutions to initiate preventative action to mitigate risk and address underlying risks by, for example, institution or type of degree.

Key Findings: Regulatory Oversight and Management of the Higher Education Sector

The recently approved legal framework for tertiary education in Kenya bodes well for improved governance of tertiary education, both institutionally and systemically. However the realization of the vision articulated by the new legislation and contingent regulations will be challenged by a lack of implementation capacity. The term "governance" is used to describe structures and processes of decision-making. In Kenya, governance of the tertiary education sector has been significantly altered through the passing of the Universities Act, 2012. The Act was introduced in alignment with the principles of the 2010 Constitution and the government's Vision 2030, with the aim to "invest in the people of Kenya" through the provision of globally competitive and quality education, training, and research to support the national developmental priorities. The Act seeks to balance measures to strengthen the autonomy of universities, while asserting accountability mechanisms, including, *inter alia*, the inclusion of non-governmental stakeholders in the governing boards, improved institutional strategic planning, performance contracting, external quality assurance, and external financial audit. The Universities Act has several commending features; notably it has:

- *Established a unified and consistent legal framework for the governance of the sector as whole.* The new Universities Act 2012 is the successor to all previous higher education legislation, including the establishing Acts for public universities and regulatory bodies, such as the Commission for Higher Education (now CUE);
- *Leveled the playing field for public and private institutions by removing the legislated dichotomy for the establishment of, quality assurance mechanisms for, and management of public and private universities;*
- *Subjected public universities to external quality assurance mechanisms;*
- *Introduced a new agency to promote financing for public higher education.* The University Fund Board will be responsible for advising the government with regard to matters relating to the funding of university education, and has been mandated to manage a fund to assist with the financing of universities. The Fund will improve the probability of objectiveness in decision making, and help to optimize merit-based funding in support of public higher education in Kenya; and

- *Changed the system wherein the senior management of public universities and administrative/regulatory bodies were directly appointed by government. The Act has introduced new mechanisms promoting open, competitive, and merit based appointment methodologies.* However, a number of members of government are still appointed to councils on an ex-officio basis, with the remaining non-government members subject to final confirmation by the Cabinet Secretary.

The passing of the Universities Act in 2012 should form the basis of a significant positive realignment in Kenya's tertiary education system; but the success of reforms initiated by the Act, and the effectiveness of changes to governance systems and structures affecting Kenyan tertiary education will be underpinned by key stakeholders to the system addressing the following five critical challenges:

Implementation of new legislation in the word and spirit intended. It takes a path breaking government and bureaucracy to reduce its influence, and build democratic practices through reliance on incentives and indirect mechanisms to assert accountability. In order for these new structures and systems to function effectively, new and substantial capacity will need to be built in administrative agencies, such as CUE for quality assurance, the University Funding Board for objective financing, and perhaps even more importantly stronger leadership, improved capacity and the development of new practices in governing bodies (university councils) and other structures to promote effective university management.

Increase the availability information at the program, institutional and national level to promote performance and financial accountability. The promotion of transparency and the use of benchmarking are important tools to advance institutional and systemic self-improvement and accountability.

Training institutional leadership. The Act created twelve new public universities, with new governing bodies and leadership teams which will require leadership and management training to ensure their effectiveness.

The application of one universal tuition fee for all government-supported students, despite differential unit costs. In the current system, students pay the same fees regardless of their course of study. For example, the fees levied on students for a degree in the social sciences are the same as those levied on students enrolled in medical degrees, despite the enormous differential in the cost of delivering these types of programs. The application of universal fees distorts institutional incentives, and promotes enrollment in low-costs programs, which may be poorly aligned with labor market trends and national developmental needs.

Lack of institutional autonomy and capacity to institute differentiated faculty remuneration at public universities. The application of a universal remuneration policy for all faculty, with limited sensitivity to the quality of teaching and research delivered, and other performance criteria, serves as a disincentive for faculty performance, and ultimately drains the system of academic talent, compromising the overall quality of university education.

Policy Options

While the Kenyan higher education system has accrued considerable gains through the expansion of tertiary enrollment, the findings summarized above demonstrate how rapid expansion has placed significant strain on the system, in a manner that could ultimately jeopardize the progress already made. This section outlines a set of ideas on policy and administrative interventions, and a potential program of investment, to mitigate these pressures. The following sections provide further detail regarding challenges facing the sector, and associated policy options.

Expanded Enrollment with Quality Educational Service Delivery

Expand the provision of STEM related programs, with a focus on concurrently improving the quality of STEM education. The delivery of STEM programming should effectively integrate classroom learning with research, and must equip graduates with technical competencies required by the sector.

Expand regional and national offerings of Masters and PhD programs. The government's goal of producing at least 1,000 PhDs per year is critical to support the expansion of the sector and the promotion of quality higher education. Improving postgraduate output will be necessity to build future faculty staff components, with adequate academic qualifications; and to support the development of a private sector with the capacity to undertake scientific and technological research and development. The GOK should collaborate with partners in Eastern and Southern Africa to scale-up the supply of quality postgraduate programming, and promote competition in the subsector. Regional partnerships could also be leveraged to endow a scholarship fund to promote quality on a cost-effective basis. Such a program of action would promote Africa-centric quality postgraduate scholarship through economies-of-scale, and should be carried out in collaboration with international partners, based on globally competitive best practices and benchmarking.

Review the attractiveness of the terms and conditions of faculty employment to ensure that they are sufficiently aligned to attract and retain the country's best academic talent. There is a concurrent need to upgrade the academic and teaching competences of existing faculty in a cost-effective manner.

Enhance the capacity of the CUE to strengthen its advisory and external quality assurance functions. If CUE is to effectively deliver on its legislated quality assurance and oversight mandates with respect to all higher education institutions, the commission will require significant capacity enhancement. CUE, and its supporting stakeholders, will need to develop and articulate a clear and viable nationwide plan to ensure effective external quality assurance at the institutional and program level.

Expanding Student Financing for Low- and Middle-Income Students

A well-functioning student loan scheme requires a capacitated and efficient system across the loan cycle—from the point wherein a student applies for a loan, to the attainment of a quality education inclusive of financial literacy, to the effective application of repayment practices premised on beneficiary income status.

Increase government financing to assist low-income students to effectively finance higher education. It is encouraging that a larger number of Kenyans are sharing the burden of financing the higher education sector through the payment of fees for tertiary education. However, the expansion of fee regimes has not been matched by a parallel increase in support to comparatively poor students. In the absence of mitigating measures to promote equitable access to tertiary education through student loans, the levying of fees in higher education will increasingly serve as a barrier to entry for relatively poor students.

Improve the targeting of financial aid to poor students. Even in a context wherein government financial support to HELB is increased, demand for student financing is likely to exceed available funding. As a consequence it is imperative to improve the targeting of support to students who need it the most. The following recommendations should be considered:

- *Concentrating student financial support towards low-income students.* In order to address significant and growing equity concerns, the largest share of public funding in support of student financial aid should be channeled to students from comparatively poor households. This could be achieved through requiring students from comparatively high income groups, for example students from the richest 20 percent of Kenyan households, are either ineligible for student loans (unless public support for student loans is increased substantially), or that stricter criteria for lending, such as the requirement of collateral or a co-guarantor to access a loan, are applied to this group.

- *Verification of applicants' income and asset information.* HELB should consider incorporating structured mechanisms for verifying data collected through the loan application scorecard. This could be achieved through household visits to verify income, on a sample basis. Moreover, the current system for means-testing is not able to accurately capture variations in household income among loan beneficiaries. HELB should assess the weights assigned to each indicator in the scorecard to enhance the utility of the instrument in identifying and prioritizing low-income beneficiaries. Instructive examples can be drawn from the experience of administering student loan programs in Colombia and Chile, among others, and the host of social safety network programs operative in Africa.

Improving coverage through higher financial sustainability. Improving loan recovery and reducing the subsidy per student without compromising equity will enable more students to benefit from loan support. This could be pursued through, *inter alia*, risk sharing and improving loan recovery.

Risk sharing with private institutions and families. Private institutions accrue substantial benefits from financial resources derived from HELB supported students, and play an important role in educating students for employment in the professions. HELB could negotiate requiring private institutions to assume co-responsibility, in the form of a partial guarantee or an upfront co-payment, to cover the risk of loan default (as is the case in Chile and Colombia); or other mechanisms for sharing risk with private higher education providers.

Families, especially affluent families, reduce out-of-pocket expenditure in support of tertiary education through access to student loans. Parents, the extended family, or community could be asked to fully or partially guarantee loan repayment, given the expected returns associated with tertiary education, and to promote seriousness on the students in their academic studies. Requiring a co-guarantor would increase commitment on the part of students and lower the costs of financing loans to government.

Improving loan recovery. Strategies informing the administration of loans, and the mitigation of delinquency and poor repayment practices, would benefit from the timely collection of data to accurately identify key institutional and beneficiary characteristics underlying risk, such information relating to dropout rates, the relevance of education programming, and an individual's propensity to evade loan repayment.

The effective administration of student loans on a sustainable basis will require investments in improved ICT infrastructure, and the formulation and implementation of communication campaigns with students to improve financial literacy and knowledge of the functioning of the loan system. While HELB is considered an example of a comparatively effective administrator of student loans in Africa, important gains will accrue through further investment in ICT systems, ICT communication to beneficiaries, and tracking tools.

The proposed changed in the legal change of HELB to become a financial institution has worked very well for instituting of sound financial processes and competences, which is an often overlooked, but critical competence of a student loan organization.

Improving Governance through the Process of Expansion

The following policy recommendations are intended to guide policy makers as they work to harness opportunities to enhance, and mitigate challenges to, management and oversight of Kenyan tertiary education. The rapid development of, and building of capacity to utilize, new accountability tools can improve systems of governance and allow for a relaxation of the government's direct role in institutional operations.

Establish effective, stakeholder-driven governing boards through, for example, capacity-building programs promoting good governance in new universities.

Training programs could include reviews of the appropriateness of institutional income generation practices in public universities, and help to ensure the alignment fund-raising and investment activities with institutional missions. Despite the increasing contribution of innovative self-funding mechanisms for the development of university education in Kenya, a number of quality, relevance and equity concerns have arisen as the system has evolved. Following two decades of practice, there is an urgent need to review the income generation mechanisms and strategies employed by public universities. Examples of equivalent training programs are evidenced in India, U.K., and the United States.

Ensure that financial audits are carried out annually, on a timely basis, and the results thereof should be made public.

Remove the potential for conflicts of interest to arise through the dual processes of accreditation and quality assurance administered by CUE and professional bodies. The 2012 Universities Act does not adequately address the potential for conflicts of interest to arise between CUE and relevant professional bodies, and their potential to undermine quality assurance and enhancement processes. The government should facilitate consultation between all key stakeholders to the process, including the government, CUE, professional bodies and universities, with a view to establishing resilient and effective approaches to accreditation and quality assurance.

Build the capacity of administrative and regulatory agencies, notably the CUE (as mentioned above), and ensure the full operationalization of the Universities Fund and Universities Funding Board, including the development of performance-based funding instruments. The CUE will require significant capacity building to effectively deliver on its legislated mandate to ensure quality assurance and accreditation within the large and complex public university subsector, in addition to the private university subsector.

Establish a rigorous and effective Higher Education Management Information System with contingent effort to promote public access to information relating to the sector. An efficient system of data collection is urgently needed to support sector-wide management, public accountability and transparency, self-improvement, and performance-based funding.

Notes

1. While Montenegro and Patrinos' paper was published in 2014, data related to Kenya are dated 2005.
2. *Nonscience* here is defined as all other courses that do not fit into the category of agriculture, engineering, computer science, ICT, medicine, veterinary science, and other.

References

Montenegro, Claudio E. and Patrinos, Harry A. 2014. "Comparable Estimates of Returns to Schooling around the World." Policy Research Working Paper 7020, World Bank, Washington, DC.

Nganga, Gilbert. 2013. "Far-Reaching Reform as New Universities Law Is Enacted." *University World News*, June 12. http://www.universityworldnews.com/article.php?story=20130122145646505.

World Bank. 2013a. *Achieving Shared Prosperity in Kenya*. Washington, DC: World Bank.

———. 2013b. *Jobs for Shared Prosperity: Time for Action in Middle East and North Africa.* Washington, DC: World Bank.

———. 2014a. *Country Partnership Strategy for Kenya Draft.* Mimeo. Washington, DC: World Bank.

———. 2014b. *Kenya: A Supply Side Analysis of Skills for the Textile Sector.* Mimeo. Washington, DC: World Bank.

———. 2014c. *Student Financing for Tertiary Education in Kenya.* Mimeo. Washington, DC: World Bank.

———. 2014d. *Tertiary Education in Kenya.* Mimeo. Washington, DC: World Bank.

CHAPTER 2

Quality and Relevance

Objective

If Kenya is to achieve the objectives of the Government's Vision 2030—to become a newly industrialized, middle-income country, while simultaneously improving the quality of life for all Kenyans by 2030—it will be critical for the country to improve the quality and relevance of post-secondary education.[1] The objective of this policy note is to summarize the challenges confronting Kenyan policymakers as the country seeks to expand the post-secondary education system, suggest policy recommendations to mitigate these challenges, and contribute to the establishment of a higher education sector that delivers quality education on an equitable basis in alignment with the economic needs of the country.

Introduction

Kenya demonstrates significant developmental potential informed by the country's location, its human capital, a comparatively strong institutional structure and capacity. Economic growth in the country averaged four percent per annum over the course of the past decade, which is higher than in the 1980s and 1990s but comparatively lower than in SSA where growth has averaged 5 percent (including South Africa) The country is making significant strides in human development as evidenced by the achievement of almost universal access to primary education, and the tripling of secondary school graduates is likely by 2030 (World Bank 2013a). Despite these laudable achievements, four out of ten Kenyans continue to live in poverty, and the further acceleration of economic growth remains constrained by low labor productivity and poor rates of investment, undermining the country's ability to fundamentally transform the livelihoods of Kenya's people (World Bank 2014a). To achieve the objective of eliminating extreme poverty by 2030, Kenya will need to reduce poverty by two percent each year until 2030 (World Bank 2014).

A persistent mismatch of skills in the labor market and low labor productivity continue to undermine private sector development. Private sector companies face significant difficulties in recruiting workers with the types of skills they demand at all levels of post-secondary education (McKinsey Global Institute 2012). In general the higher education sector has failed to tailor programs in alignment with shifting demand in the labor market, and continues to deliver courses premised on outdated curricula. As a result, employers consistently complain that graduates do not have adequate skills to fulfil the tasks demanded of them. Current higher education programming is unaligned with the developmental trajectory of the Kenyan economy, with significant gaps evident in subjects taught and disciplines offered (Mburu 2014). These challenges are also evident in the delivery of technical and vocational education and training (TVET) (World Bank 2014b).

The current expansion of Kenyan post-secondary education is in part a response to demographic change, as well as pressures generated by reforms that successfully expanded access to primary and secondary education. The success of interventions to expand access to, and improve the quality of education delivered, in the primary and secondary sectors has expanded the cohort of young people ready to enter post-secondary education. Enrollment in primary education almost doubled from approximately six million to ten million between 2001 and 2013, while the number of students enrolled in secondary education more than doubled over the same period, from 760,000 in 2001 to over two million today (Kenyan Economic Survey, various years). A growing youth population has increased the pressure on the government of Kenya (GoK) to expand post-secondary educational opportunities in both the university and TVET sub-sectors.

The rapid growth of the post-secondary sector has generated significant systemic stress. Over the course of the past five years, the number of Kenyan universities and university enrollment has doubled. It is expected that the TVET sector is will follow a similar path in response to demographic pressures and the new constitutional imperative that each of the country's 47 counties acquire a TVET institution. The GOK is in the process of implementing a number of reforms to strengthen the delivery of post-secondary education, including the implementation of the Universities Act of 2012 and the TVET ACT of 2013. A third Act is established the Kenya Qualification Authority which will be responsible for developing a National Qualifications Framework (NQF). These reforms will dovetail with plans to devolve the administration of post-secondary education, with implications for the management of the sector.

Kenya faces both opportunities and risks as it expands post-secondary education. Improving the quality of Kenyan human capital has the potential to improve the employment prospects of a burgeoning youth population, in turn increasing the number of Kenyans with stable high-income jobs and the creation of a growing and stable middle class. The cumulative impact of these outcomes would improve national economic output and decrease the dependency ratio. However, experience from other countries demonstrates that the rapid expansion of education systems can go awry when the process of systemic expansion neglects to focus on the maintenance and enhancement of educational quality and relevance. Sub-optimal outcomes associated with such a course of action include the expansion of qualifications with limited relevance and/or of poor quality, which compromise the employability of graduates, and the inequitable expansion of the system in such a way that the educational opportunities for poor and marginalized populations are compromised.

This policy note will analyze existing and potential challenges facing Kenya as it continues to expand the post-secondary education system. Section 1 examines demographic challenges, and the implications of successful government interventions that have expanded access to primary and secondary education in Kenya. The note then focusses on risks associated with the rapid expansion of post-secondary education systems. Section 2 examines challenges associated with ensuring that post-secondary education is sufficiently relevant to the needs of the economy, and to what extent Kenya is likely to achieve an appropriate balance of qualifications. Section 3 focusses on the extent to which the Kenyan post-secondary system is positioned to ensure sufficient quality in the delivery of qualifications. Section 4 focusses on faculty resources and associated challenges, while Section 5 examines the challenge of ensuring equity as the system expands.

The Youth Bulge and the Expected Tsunami of Secondary Educated Graduates

As is the case in many developing countries, Kenya has a significant youth bulge; evidence of an ongoing demographic transition. In 2013, approximately 26 million of Kenya's inhabitants, equivalent to half of the population, were below the age of 25. The share of 25 year old inhabitants is projected to rise to two thirds of a total population of 63 million by 2030 (World Bank 2014). Kenya's labor force is projected to double by 2045, with the majority of the working age population concentrated in urban areas (World Bank 2013a). As a consequence of an ongoing demographic transition, Kenya's dependency ratio is declining. However, for the foreseeable future the population of the country will continue to grow due to the lagging effects of high fertility rates. Kenya's youth bulge can be catalyzed into a significant productive resource with a significant developmental dividend, if the country is able to effectively skill and employ rising numbers of entrants to the labor force.

Kenya has rolled out a series of reforms for primary and secondary education and has initiated a program of investment in human capital with a focus on youth. In 2003, the GOK implemented a policy of free primary education, and in 2008 implemented a complementary policy for free secondary education. The first cohort of students to benefit from the expansion of free primary education in 2003 will commence completing a full cycle of secondary education in 2015. The large number of youth expected to exit the schooling system in 2015 seeking entry to post-secondary education is commonly referred to as a "Youth Tsunami." Figure 2.1 illustrates enrollment figures for primary and secondary education between 2001 and 2013.[2] While primary enrollment rose from 7.2 million in 2003, the first year of free primary education, to over 10.1 million

Figure 2.1 Enrollment in Primary and Secondary Education in Kenya, 2001–13

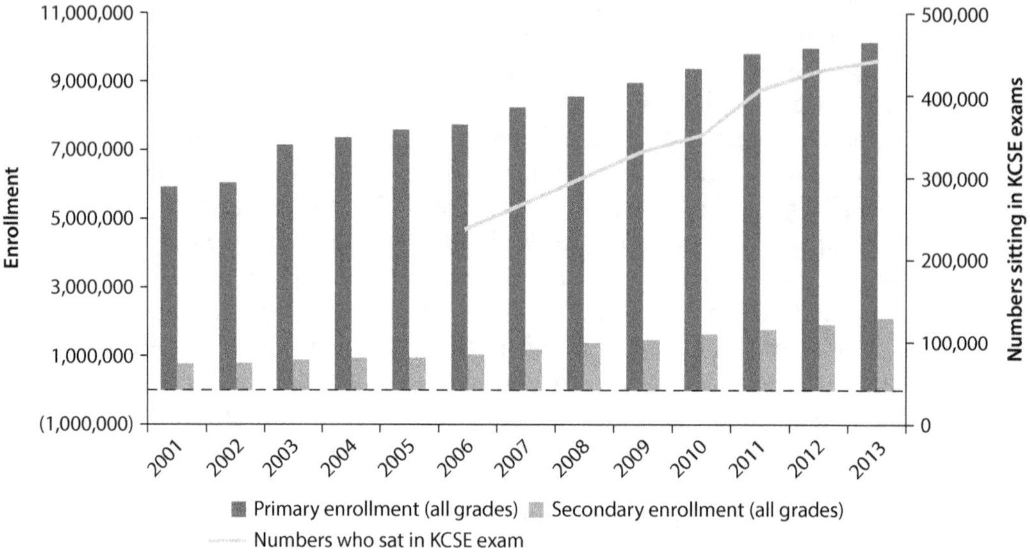

■ Primary enrollment (all grades)   ■ Secondary enrollment (all grades)
— Numbers who sat in KCSE exam

Source: Kenya Bureau of Statistics, various years.
Note: KCSE = Kenya Certificate of Secondary Education.

in 2013, equivalent to a forty percent increase in enrollment, enrollment in secondary education increased by fifty percent since the introduction of free secondary education, from 1.4 million in 2008 to 2.1 million in 2013 (HELB data).

In the five years spanning 2008 and 2013, the number of students sitting the Kenya Certificate of Secondary Education (KCSE) for matriculation from secondary education, increased by almost fifty percent. The introduction of free secondary education is linked to an improvement in the number of students transitioning from primary to secondary education, which rose from 60 percent in 2008 to 73 percent in 2013. Rising transition rates are linked to a concurrent increase in the number of students sitting the KCSE exams, which rose from 301,000 in 2008 to 445,000 in 2013. The increase in the number of students sitting the KCSE between 2008 and 2013 is equivalent to 47 percent; marginally below the fifty percent increase in secondary enrollment over the same period. The number of KCSE matriculates who achieved the grade of C+ required for entry into university education has increased by 70.3 percent, from 72,649 in 2008 to 123,704 in 2012.

Analysis of the rates of return for different levels of education in Kenya, while dated, suggest that higher levels of education are associated with higher returns to education.[3] Using data from the 2005 Household Survey (HHS), the rate of return associated with tertiary education in Kenya was calculated at 22.4 percent, with concurrent rates of return to tertiary education for men of 21.2 percent and women of 24.9 percent (Montenegro and Patrinos 2014). The rates of return for tertiary education in Kenya are generally aligned with Montenegro and

Patrinos' (2014) thesis that for all levels of education, rates of return to education in sub-Saharan Africa are highest for tertiary education.

However, research demonstrates that rates of return to education vary by the quality of the skills learnt or acquired. Labor markets demonstrably reward individuals with relevant skills, over years spent in the education system as an end in itself. Haushek and Wößmann (2007) have demonstrated that the quality of cognitive skills acquired by an individual through education is a more important determinant of individual earnings, distribution of income and economic growth, than years spent in schooling. Evidence from the United States of America (USA) demonstrates that individuals who obtain a college education without acquiring a specific set of skills are associated with low returns to education (Ingram and Newmann 2006). Moreover, recent analysis indicates that rates of return to education vary by non-cognitive ability, underlining the importance of non-cognitive skills—such as persistence, motivation and emotional stability—as important complements to education and skills acquisition (see Lindqvist and Vestman 2011). In order to reap the full demographic dividend of Kenya's youth bulge it will be critical to equip this generation of youth with quality skills relevant to the needs of the labor market. If imparted skills and training do not stimulate economic opportunities, the economic benefits associated with post-secondary education will not materialize.

Evidence suggests that Kenyan firms struggle to recruit workers with appropriate skills. The World Bank's Enterprise Survey for Kenya (2013) reported that 28.9 percent of firms surveyed stated an inadequately skilled workforce as their most important constraint inhibiting growth. Other evidence suggests that Kenya's post-secondary qualifications are not adequately skilling young people, and that some graduates are unable to find jobs due to their poor skills sets, despite the achievement of tertiary qualifications (Mburu 2014).

Limited Relevance of Programs

As Kenya's post-secondary education system expands, it will be critical to ensure that students are channeled into programs aligned with the needs of the labor market. In contexts in which demand for post-secondary education exceeds supply, it often observed that tertiary institutions continue to supply and expand existing programs and qualifications, as opposed to introducing new or modified programs in response to shifting demand in the economy, contributing to a skills mismatch. Modifying education and training systems in response to changing economic conditions is challenging due its dependence on mechanisms to effectively channel labor market information to institutions of learning, and is further complicated in contexts wherein signals from the market with regard to the relevance of education are weak or absent.

A key challenge in this regard will be to ensure that the Kenyan post-secondary system offers an appropriate suite of professional short courses, TVET and university qualifications that balance the holistic needs of the economy. Historically, TVET qualifications have been perceived to be less prestigious, and of lower value, than university qualifications. As a consequence TVET qualifications often attract less demand; even in contexts in which there is evidence of healthy returns (wages) to TVET education. There is a tendency on the part of governments to perpetuate imbalance in the provision of post-secondary qualifications through the over-supply of—often comparatively irrelevant—university degrees, at the expense investing in TVET programming and undertaking outreach programs to convince students enrolling in post-secondary education of the value of TVET qualifications.

Evidence suggests that countries that have successfully transitioned from low- to middle-income status, and in turn from middle- to high-income status, have appropriately balanced academic and professional qualifications. The governments of middle-income countries in East Asia prioritized TVET qualifications as evidenced by the share of TVET enrollment as a share of total tertiary enrollment in these countries. In 2007, for example, 50 percent of tertiary students in China were enrolled in TVET, with equivalent TVET enrollment of 60 percent in Malaysia and a little less than 50 percent the Republic of Korea. Korea and China, moreover, have prioritized TVET in the upper secondary sub-cycle of education (World Bank 2012).

The number of Kenyan students enrolled in TVET programs has increased in recent years, and the current proposed reforms for the TVET sector will further prioritize the subsector. However, as is illustrated in figure 2.2, the share of TVET enrollment as a share of total enrollment in tertiary education has decreased relative to university enrollment. In 2005, TVET enrollment accounted for 47 percent of total post-secondary enrollment; however, in 2013 the share

Figure 2.2 Changes in Kenyan Post-Secondary Enrollment: TVET and Universities

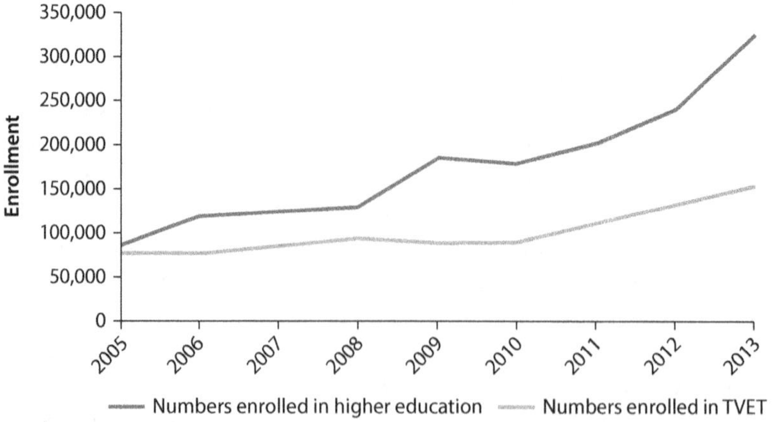

Source: Kenya National Bureau of Statistics, various years.
Note: Data only captures enrollment for TVET and technical institutions managed by MoEST (excluding youth polytechnics). MoEST = Ministry of Education, Science and Technology; TVET = technical and vocational education and training.

of TVET enrollment in total tertiary enrollment had fallen to 31 percent. The GOK's goal is to achieve a gross enrollment ratio (GER) of 30 percent in TVET by 2030 (Republic of Kenya 2012).

Consistent with a trend evident in many SSA countries, Kenyan students demonstrate relatively poor enrollment in science, technology, engineering, and math (STEM) courses. Between 2005 and 2010, the majority of undergraduate students in Kenyan universities were enrolled in nonscience-related courses.[4] In 2005 enrollment in nonscience programs accounted for 80 percent of all Kenyan undergraduates, with a slight decline to 78 percent by 2010 (see table 2.1). Through the course of the past decade there has been a small but increasing trend in enrollment in engineering-, medicine-, and agricultural-related courses. The concentration of enrollment in nonscience-related courses is in part associated with the ease and comparatively low cost of delivering these programs relative to STEM programs, and due to the fact that universities make money from these programs. Nonscience subjects, for example, do not require the often expensive labs and equipment required to effectively deliver a STEM program, and the quality of nonscience courses delivered is less likely to be compromised by increases in class size.

The large proportion of enrollment concentrated in nonscience-related programs may be associated with high rates of graduate underemployment. In Tunisia, for example, evidence suggests that graduates from technical fields are more likely to find employment in the field in which they have been trained compared to graduates from the social sciences. A recent World Bank study found that three-and-a-half years following graduation almost 60 percent of Tunisian humanities and law graduates were employed below their level of qualification, compared to less than one percent for graduates in the disciplines of medicine, telecommunication and electricity (World Bank 2013b).

Policy Recommendations

To ensure the relevancy of post-secondary programs, the following policy recommendations are proposed:

Table 2.1 Undergraduate Enrollment in Science-Related Disciplines as a Proportion of Total Undergraduate Enrollment in Kenyan Universities
percent

	2005	2006	2007	2008	2009	2010
Agriculture	6	7	8	8	7	6
Engineering	7	6	7	8	9	8
Computer science, ICT	2	2	2	3	2	2
Medicine	4	4	4	4	4	5
Veterinary science	2	2	2	2	1	1
Nonscience	80	79	77	76	76	78

Source: Modified from table 5.7, USAID, 2013.
Note: ICT = information and communication technology.

National Qualifications Framework

The Government is in the process of aligning skills acquisition and learning with the provisions of the 2014 Kenya NQF. The Kenya Qualification Authority authorized to develop the Kenya Qualification framework, will assess the competencies of existing programs, ensuring improved skills acquisition through the delivery of existing TVET and university programs. All efforts should be directed to support this initiative and ensure that the NQF materializes quickly.

STEM Related Programming

The expansion of STEM courses in TVET and university institutions should be prioritized. While enrollment in university STEM programs is increasing, this trend should be assessed to ensure that enrollment is being channeled towards priority fields associated with Kenya's development to meet the objectives articulated in Vision 2030. It is also essential to ensure that STEM programs sufficiently balance classroom learning and research, and that graduates are equipped with the technical competencies required by the sector. Specific recommendations include:

- Strengthening science and math education in the basic and secondary cycles of education. Improved performance on the part of secondary students will encourage entry to STEM related programming in subsequent cycles of education. Complementary policies could include improving the remuneration and career trajectories of STEM teachers. Moreover, in order to address persistently low enrollment on the part of women in STEM programs, magnet programs should be established in secondary schools to mentor young girls, and to assist female students to transition to university STEM related study;
- Informing prospective students of the attractive career trajectories and remuneration associated with STEM careers;
- Establishing scholarship programs with links to internships and possible jobs for qualifying students who choose to pursue STEM related university and TVET qualifications;
- Incentivizing universities, through public funding mechanisms, to recruit more students to STEM programs and to improve graduate output in STEM related fields.

Private Sector Engagement

With a view to ensuring the alignment of program content with labor market demand, and to promote the employability of graduates, most Kenyan universities are required to engage private sector firms with regard to curricula review. However, in practice, these requirements are not met, and the process rarely works (World Bank 2014b). Universities must re-examine existing procedures for engaging the private sector, and introduce innovative mechanisms to more effectively utilize the private sector to improve the relevance of programmatic offerings and improve the transition of students into employment. This could be achieved through, *inter alia*:

- Incentivizing universities, through public funding mechanisms, to develop active research, consulting and other knowledge-based partnerships with the private sector;
- Encouraging private sector leaders to engage, through teaching assignments and other programs, universities to promote improved understanding, and potentially investment in, university programs and students;
- Target university alumni in private sector firms through information and communications campaigns to encourage the establishment active relationships between universities and private firms.

Labor Market Information System

Kenya's current system for tracking the dynamics of the labor market, the Labor Market Information System (LMIS), is weak and is undermined by poor coordination. Strengthening the LMIS will be critical to ensure that accurate labor information is shared with universities and students in timely manner.

Expansion without Quality

An effective quality assurance (QA) system is a key component for ensuring quality in higher education. QA systems need to appropriately cohere and balance the imperatives of pre-existing institutions (higher education governance and market structures), QA mechanisms (accreditation, assessment, and audit),[5] incentive structures (required or not, financing mechanisms, disclosure procedures, etc.), and the objectives of the overarching QA system (accountability vs. improvement) in order to function effectively. An additional critical component for ensuring effective QA is an assessment of institutional capacity to enforce QA. Independent results-based financing systems can play an important role in incentivizing QA compliance. Kenya is in the process of implementing important reforms to QA and financing systems with the potential to significantly improve the balance between accountability and improvements in QA. A critical challenge in this regard will be to ensure that these reforms are effectively implemented and that they keep pace with the rapid expansion of the post-secondary system.

The number of public and private universities in Kenya is expanding rapidly. In 2007 there were thirteen chartered universities comprised of six public universities and seven private universities. In 2014, the number of public chartered universities had risen to 22, with a concurrent increase in private chartered universities to 17. Moreover, in 2014 there were an additional eleven private universities holding letters of authority, and two registered private universities.[6] A number of public and private universities are disaggregated into constituent colleges, with nine colleges in public universities and five in the private subsector. While the TVET sector has not demonstrated equivalent institutional growth, the GOK plans to establish new TVET institutions in each of the 47 counties established by the 2010 Constitution.

Given the existing and continued expansion of the numbers of tertiary institutions, it will be critical that the government and its agencies ensure that new institutions deliver programs demanded by the labor market. Current data suggest that Kenyan firms struggle to recruit workers with appropriate skills (see figure 2.3). A recent McKinsey study cited one Kenyan business owner as stating that "We can easily find people [with a] tertiary education to drive trucks, but it is impossible to find anyone with a few years of accounting experience" (McKinsey 2011). A contingent challenge will be to ensure that the new regional constituent colleges of public universities, many of which are based in rural areas, do not duplicate courses delivered in urban centers and focus instead on tailoring programs relevant to local economies. It will also be important to ensure that these programs are professionally oriented, with less of a pure academic focus.

Effective implementation of the recently passed University (2012) and Technical and Vocational Education and Training Acts (2013) will play a critical role in QA. New legislation is intended to, *inter* alia, promote harmonization across the university and TVET post-secondary sectors, improve sector management, extend the mandates of existing institutions and establish new institutions for the purposes of QA and improved financial management. Implementation of the University and TVET Acts is ongoing, with varying degrees of completion.

The Universities Act of 2012 has fundamentally changed how public sector higher education institutions are managed. Under the new Act all public and private institutions will be subject to the same form of government regulation. The Commission for University Education (CUE), which previously accredited institutions and programs in private universities, is now mandated to undertake QA for the university sector as a whole. A new University Fund has been

Figure 2.3 Percentage of Firms in Kenya Identifying an Inadequately Educated Workforce as a Major Constraint

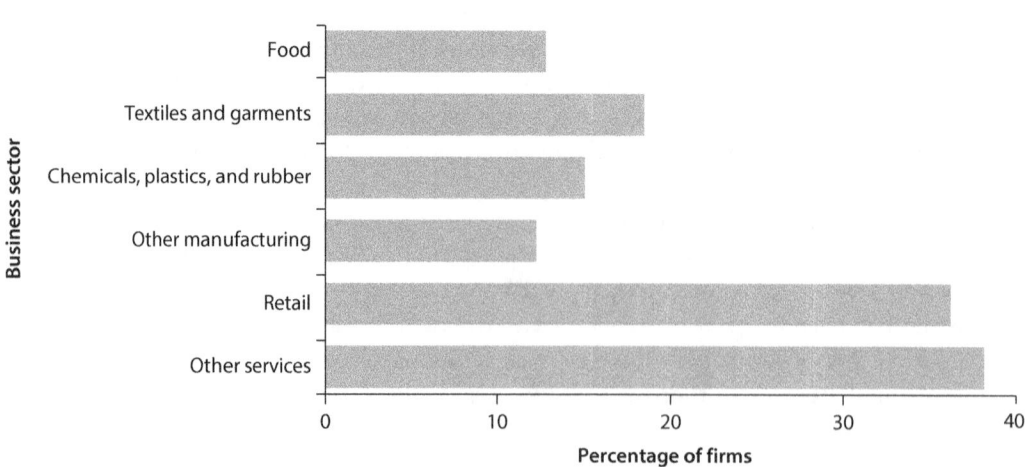

Source: World Bank Enterprise Survey for Kenya, 2013.

established to phase out the use of public subsidies to universities, and replace them with funding premised on the unit costs of programs offered, differentiated remuneration for faculty, and other criteria to be prioritized by the Fund. A third body established by the Act, the Kenya University and College Central Placement Services (KUCCPS) will be responsible for admitting students to both public and private universities, financed out of the public purse (Republic of Kenya 2012).

The challenge for newly established bodies mandated with the responsibility to ensuring QA compliance will be significant in light of capacity and resource constraints. The CUE's extended mandate includes the accreditation of all public universities and their programs. In 2013, the year following the implementation of the University ACT, CUE was able to accredit the seven public universities. Currently CUE must still accredit 23 constituent colleges in the public subsector, and all new private universities that have received a letter of interim authority. Moreover, if the CUE is to fulfil its entire mandate as envisioned by the Act, it will also need to accredit all programs at universities. The University of Nairobi alone has 371 programs. The institutional capacity of CUE will require further strengthening if it is to fulfil the role assigned to it.

The Technical and Vocational Education and Training Act of 2013 was passed to restructure the TVET subsector in line with equivalent measures outlined in the Universities Act (2012). A new Technical and Vocational Education and Training Authority (TVETA) has been established by the TVET Act with the responsibility to harmonize, organize, accredit and register institutions. Given the highly fragmented structure of TVET delivery in Kenya, TVETA will face significant challenges in delivering on its mandate in accordance with the Act.[7] In line with the provisions of the Universities Act, the TVET Act also requires the establishment of a new body entitled the Technical and Vocational Education and Training Curriculum Development, Assessment and Certification Council, and a new TVET Funding board. A Kenya Qualification Authority was established in 2014 to develop a NQF for Kenya. Ensuring the implementation of these Acts through their envisioned implementing agencies will require significant capacity enhancement to empower these new institutions.

The QA system will need to be particularly vigilant through the process of institutional expansion, as informational asymmetries prevail between consumers and producers of higher education. CUE and TVETA will require a well-integrated and effective Higher Education Management Information System (HEMIS) with the capacity to generate timely and accurate reports to effectively deliver on their QA mandates.

Faculty staff components have not kept pace with the expansion of enrollment in the TVET and university sectors. Definitive data is unavailable, but anecdotal evidence suggests that increases in the number of students have not been matched by equivalent increases in faculty resources. Nganga estimates that while Kenyan student numbers more than doubled over the course of the past five years, the concurrent increase in faculty numbers has only been 28.6 percent, from 7,000 to 9,000 members of staff (Nganga 2013). Anecdotal evidence suggests that is not uncommon for faculty to work in up to eight or nine institutions at a time.

Statistics on student-teacher ratios (STR) underline increasing stress on faculty resources as the system expands. Data provided by CUE with regard to STR in the 22 chartered institutions in 2014, demonstrates an average STR of 36:1 in the Kenyan higher education sector, but with significant variance. Within the system, STRs range from a low of 14:1 at the Technical University of Kenya and 17:1 at the South Eastern University of Kenya, to a high of high 64:1 at Kenyatta University, 63:1 at Laikipia University and 60:1 at Kisii University. (Source: World Bank 2010)

Available evidence suggests significant variance in STR's by university department, with particularly high STRs in the humanities and social sciences. Detailed data from the University of Nairobi, reported by Gudo, Olel, and Oanda demonstrates STRs of 92:1 in education and external studies, and 49:1 in the humanities and social sciences, compared to 26:1 in the departments of architecture and engineering. At Masinde Muliro University STRs range from a high of 52:1 in education and the social sciences to 16:1 in engineering, and a low of 7:1 in the sciences (Gudo, Olel, and Oanda 2011).

Policy Recommendations

To ensure that the quality of education programs delivered is not compromised through the process of expanding post-secondary education in Kenya, the following policies should be considered:

Expand local Master's and PhD programs and postgraduate enrollment: The expansion of universities and TVET institutions will require a complementary expansion in the supply of faculty to staff new and existing institutions. There is a concurrent need to upgrade the skills of existing faculty. STRs in Kenya are relatively high in the context of the region, particularly in the social sciences. One means for increasing the supply of workers with the skills required to fill faculty positions would be to increase the number of Master's and PhD programs and program capacity in the country and region. This would not only help to ensure that aspirant faculty remain in country and do not became part of the diaspora, but PhD students could be retained or required to teach undergraduate classes while they work towards their qualifications. Specific interventions in this regard could include the following:

- Capacitating and supporting new initiatives such as the Korean funded Kenyan Advanced Institute for Science and Technology (KAIST), which focusses on expanding the pool of STEM Master's and PhDs candidates, through the provision of additional resources and technical support.
- Focusing on establishing centers of excellence through participation in the World Bank's Eastern and Southern Higher Education Centers of Excellence project, which aims to upgrade existing institutions with the intention of strengthening applied research and training in priority areas in support of African economic development.

Review the attractiveness of faculty working conditions and remuneration: In order to make the teaching profession in the tertiary sector attractive to new graduates, it will be critical to evaluate the working conditions and remuneration prevalent the sector and ensure that pay-scales and benefits are sufficiently competitive relative to the private sector.

Integrate performance indicators and incentives into faculty contracts: Faculty should be incentivized to improve their teaching practices, undertake quality research and publish their research findings. Incentives should be structured through the contracting process to align improved performance with monetary benefits.

Establish and enhance the capacity of new regulatory and funding bodies: The human and institutional capacity (data systems, computers, software etc.) of the CUE and TVETA will need to be strengthened to ensure that they can effectively deliver on their statutory mandates. There is a concurrent need to assess the capacity and adequacy of existing QA systems, and assess the extent to which existing systems need to be strengthened to tackle challenges associated with an expanding post-secondary system. It will be critical to align new regulatory and funding bodies to ensure a collective and complementary approach towards meeting sector-wide objectives.

Establish HEMIS: The availability of accurate, real-time data on the functioning of the higher education system will be critical for ensuring relevance and quality in programs delivered. At present, no single entity is responsible for the maintenance of higher education or TVET sector databases, and regulatory bodies such as CUE do not have accurate information about enrollment in institutions and programs. Moreover, accurate information with regard to graduate output and rates of dropouts is negligible. As the system expands, the institutionalization of mechanisms to ensure regular system-wide and institutional data collection will be critical to promote effective sector-wide management and to promote accountability and transparency.

Inequitable Expansion

As the post-secondary system expands, it runs the risk of failing to equalize opportunities for key disadvantaged constituents such as women, rural populations and the poor. If the quality of education is compromised, the provision of comparatively irrelevant qualifications will undermine the potential returns accruing to education. Poor student financing mechanisms in support of post-secondary education undermine opportunities for low income students to access post-secondary education. Specific barriers to entry for particular groups, such as women, may require system-wide interventions to equalize opportunities.

The provision of relatively irrelevant post-secondary qualifications and/or qualifications of a poor quality can worsen existing inequalities. The poorest and most marginalized populations in many cases have access to the worst quality of public service provision. The quality and relevance of qualification may also vary by geographical location and can reinforce existing spatial disparities. Academic institutions that are located in more affluent, or urban, regions are more likely benefit from better facilities, faculty and quality students, and as a consequence are more likely to deliver quality educational services. Institutions located in comparatively affluent areas are also more likely to accrue indirect benefits due to their proximity to growth nodes (clusters of firms, financial districts etc.). In an effort to address existing spatial inequity, plans to expand post-secondary education in Kenya include measures to establish 33 satellite campuses for Kenya's primary public universities (the University of Nairobi, Kenyatta University etc.) in rural areas. While these interventions represent a significant opportunity for expanding access to post-secondary education for people concentrated in historically marginalized parts of the country, if satellite campuses deliver education of comparatively poor quality, they are likely to perpetuate existing spatial inequalities rather than narrowing the urban-rural divide.

The costs associated with post-secondary education can constitute a significant barrier to entry, particularly for aspirant students from poor and marginalized communities. It is likely that costs will become a more significant consideration if public institutions raise fees in response to declining government subsidies; if the expansion of post-secondary enrollment is primarily accommodated in the private subsector; and/or if financing in support of student loans decreases relative to rising enrollment. As part of the GOK's plans to reform student financing, and to introduce tuition differentiated by institution and program, the current fee system as applied in Kenyan universities is due to undergo a review in 2014. While the number of students in private institutions has grown substantially in the past five years, the majority of new university placements in response rising enrollment have been accommodated in public universities. A significant challenge with regard to improving equity and equalizing opportunities for post-secondary education will arise through the process of ensuring that Kenya's student loan financing scheme managed by the Higher Education Loan Board (HELB) expands on a sustainable basis in alignment with the rising numbers of students entering post-secondary education.

Systems that effectively and sustainably target student loans to marginal and poorer student populations play an important role in overcoming equity challenges (Salmi and Bassett, forthcoming). Available evidence suggests that the current Kenyan system for administering student loans is able to target students relatively effectively. HELB's targeting instrument evaluates applicants against a set of criteria to determine who receives a loan, and how much they receive in financial assistance. HELB's mean targeting instrument allocates loans in proportion to the income group of the loan applicant. However, as figure 2.4 illustrates, the variation in mean loans by income group is relatively small. Available data suggests that the average HELB loan extended to successful applicants from the lowest income group (those who earn less than KSh 20,000) is only 20 percent higher than that received by successful applicants from the highest income group (those who earn more than KSh 150,000).

Figure 2.4 Average Loans per Income Group

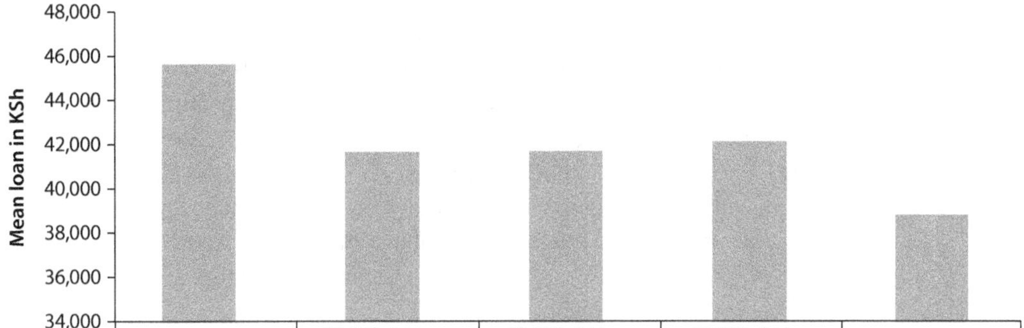

	hhinc<20,000	20,000<hhinc<40,000	40,000<hhinc<60,000	60,000<hhinc<150,000	hhinc>150,000
Mean loan	45,629.92	41,652.02	41,676.48	42,115.87	38,795.71

Source: HELB Data quoted in World Bank 2014c.
Note: HELB = Higher Education Loan Board; hhinc = household income; KSh = Kenyan shillings.

Kenya's existing loan scheme faces a number of challenges with the capacity to undermine its ability to equalize opportunities. As the number of students entering post-secondary education increases, the biggest challenge facing HELB will be to bridge the gap between the availability of funds to support student financing and demand for student loans. For example, in 2013/2014 HELB was expected to disburse student loans to a value of KSh 6.94 billion, against a government allocation of KSh 2.67 billion (KSh 14.5 billion had been requested), and loan recovery of KSh 2.54 billion; resulting in an annualized funding gap of KSh 1.73 billion.

Policy Recommendations

To ensure that the expansion of post-secondary enrollment addresses issues of inclusivity and equity, the following policy recommendations should be considered:

Student Financing: Effectively targeted student financing, of sufficient magnitude, is critical for mitigating financial barriers to entry, and for expanding opportunities for post-secondary education to comparatively poor students. Currently HELB, the entity responsible for student financing in Kenya, is struggling to extend targeted finance to the increasing numbers of secondary graduates aspiring to enter the post-secondary system, and not all qualifying students can be supported. A number of policy interventions should be considered to improve the targeting of poor and marginal students, improve the system for loan recovery, ensure the development of alternative sources of funding for HELB, and to ensure the financial sustainability of the student loan financing system. The policy note on student financing included in this report provides further detail on proposed policy interventions.

Strengthening of new institutions: The primary rationale informing the establishment of constituent colleges within the public university subsector, was to improve the provision of post-secondary education for aspirant students in rural and marginalized areas. In the past, the expansion of post-secondary opportunities has often been achieved through the upgrading of existing technical and vocational institutions in targeted regions. In many instances, despite upgrading, these institutions remained poorly equipped and under-resourced. New regional institutions will require significant investment to ensure that they are capable of delivering university level programming of a comparable educational standard to that delivered at the main campuses of publicly chartered universities and in accordance with CUE standards.

Hold institutions accountable for dropout and completion rates: To improve operational efficiencies, and to optimize the returns for public investments in higher education, institutions of higher learning need to be incentivized to improve performance. This can be achieved through the linking of institutional funding to key outcome indicators, including an assessment of student performance by category (for example, students drawn from lower income groups and/or marginalized communities, graduate output, and rates of dropout). Such a course of action would motivate institutions to establish remedial programs to support students at greater risk of dropping out.

Conclusion

The GOK's stated objective to improve the livelihoods of all Kenyans and for achieving middle-income status by 2030 are fundamentally linked to the need to investment in educating and training the Kenyan people. Key policy interventions in support of free primary and secondary education have increased the number of years of educational attainment for the average Kenyan worker, and more students are ready to take advantage of opportunities for post-secondary education and the higher salaries associated with it.

The GOK is currently implementing plans to significantly expand post-secondary education provision in response to rapidly increasing numbers of secondary students seeking entry to the post-secondary system. The implementation of associated reforms at the university level has resulted in the number of public and private institutions more than doubling in the last five years with a concurrent fifty percent increase in university enrollment. Moreover, due to the passing of the 2013 TVET Act, a number of similar reforms are expected to be rolled out in the TVET sector.

As the Government navigates the process of post-secondary expansion, a number of challenges will need to be addressed to mitigate risks with the potential to compromise the quality and relevance of future graduates. If institutions, programs and university enrollment are expanded without due consideration for aligning new programs, skills and increased graduate output with demand in the labor market, the contribution of post-secondary expansion to national development could be regressive. In light of these challenges, it is concerning that the proportion of higher education enrollment accruing to TVET programs has declined in recent years. In order to ensure that the post-secondary sector effectively contributes to achieving Kenya's growth objectives, the expansion of the sector will also need to take into account the alignment of subjects taken by graduates with developmental priorities. An additional risk associated with a rapid expansion of post-secondary enrollment with the potential to compromise the quality of education delivered, is that increases in the supply of infrastructure and faculty does not keep pace with rising enrollment. Lastly, efforts to expand access to post-secondary education must adequately weigh equity considerations to ensure that marginalized groups benefit from the process.

Measures must be taken to mitigate these and associated risks to ensure that an expanded post-secondary education sector retains and strengthens its relevance, that the quality of education delivered is maintained and improved, and that measures to promote equity are protected and strengthened. This short policy note undertook a quick assessment of challenges facing Kenya as it moves to expand its post-secondary system, and has proposed a number of policy recommendations with the potential to mitigate these risks.

Notes

1. Vision 2030 is the national development plan which aims to transform Kenya into a newly industrializing middle-income country while concurrently improving the quality life of all citizens. It is based on three key pillars focused on economic, social and political outcomes, and aims to attain an annual GDP growth rate of 10 percent per annum by 2030.
2. Data for 2013 is provisional.
3. Analysis of rates of return to different levels of education in Kenya are drawn from 2005, the last year in which a household survey was undertaken. A new household survey was undertaken in 2014 which will allow for new calculations.
4. *Nonscience* here is defined as all other courses that do not fit into the category of agriculture, engineering, computer science, ICT, medicine, and veterinary science.
5. *Accreditation* refers to a process in which a government or private body evaluates the quality of a higher education institution as a whole or of a specific education program, in order to formally recognize it as having met certain predetermined criteria or standards. The result of the process is usually the awarding of a status (yes/no decision) of recognition.

    Assessment refers to a process of gathering, quantifying and using information towards assessing the instructional effectiveness and adequacy of curricula delivered by higher education institutions as a whole or of its programs.

    Audit refers to the process of reviewing an institution or a program with a focus on accountability with respect to stated aims and objectives (Vlasceanu et al, 2004).
6. Universities with charters have met the Commission of University Education (CUE)'s standards for a fully functioning university. Private universities operating with Letters of Interim Authority (LIA) from CUE continue to receive guidance and direction to continue developing resources and facilities towards full university accreditation (Award of Charter). Institutions operating under LIA's are allowed to admit students

to approved programs. Registered private universities are a special category which predate the establishment of CUE, and the earlier body it has replaced, the Commission for Higher Education. These institutions are still pending the award of a charter. See CUE's webpage for further detail. http://www.cue.or.ke/services/accreditation/status-of-universities.

7. Currently, within the MoEST, there are 48 existing institutions in the TVET sector and a further 34 institutions undergoing establishment. The Ministry of Labor and Human Resource Development manages five TVET institutions, and a further 697 Youth Polytechnics are managed by the Ministry of Youth Affairs. Another 87 institutions are managed by 15 other ministries and there are over 1,000 institutions in the non-government sector, including those privately owned (Republic of Kenya 2012).

References

Gudo, Calleb, Olel, Maureen, and Oanda, Ibrahim. 2011. "University Expansion in Kenya and Issues of Quality Education: Challenges and Opportunities." *International Journal of Business and Social Science* 2 (2).

Haushek, Eric A., and Ludger Wößmann. 2007. "The Role of Education Quality for Economic Growth." Policy Research Working Paper 4122, World Bank, Washington, DC.

Ingram, B., and Newmann, G. 2006. "The Returns to Skill." *Labor Economics* 13 (1): 35–59.

Lindqvist, E., and Vestman, R. 2011. "The Labor Market Returns to Cognitive and Non-Cognitive Ability: Evidence from Swedish Enlistment." *American Economic Journal* 3: 101–28.

Mburu, Kinuthia. 2014. "Labour Crisis: Widening Skills Gap Costs Local Graduates Jobs." Accessed on June 6, 2014, from *The Daily Nation*. http://mobile.nation.co.ke/lifestyle/Widening-skills-gap-costs-local-graduates-jobs/-/1950774/2291248/-/format/xhtml/-/efotb9/-/index.html.

McKinsey Global Institute. 2012. *Africa at Work: Job Creation and Inclusive Growth*. http://www.mckinsey.com/global-themes/middle-east-and-africa/africa-at-work#0.

Montenegro, Claudio E., and Patrinos, Harry A. 2014. "Comparable Estimates of Returns to Schooling around the World." Policy Research Working Paper 7020, World Bank, Washington, DC.

Nganga, Gilbert. 2013. "Far-Reaching Reform as New Universities Law Is Enacted." *University World News*, June 12. http://www.universityworldnews.com/article.php?story=20130122145646505.

Republic of Kenya. 2012. *Universities Act*. Kenya Gazette Supplement. Government of Kenya, Nairobi. http://kenyalaw.org/kl/fileadmin/pdfdownloads/Acts/TheUniversitiesAct2012.PDF.

Salmi, J., and Bassett, R. M. (unpublished). *Opportunities for All: A Global Study on Equity and Tertiary Education*. Washington, DC: World Bank.

USAID (U.S. Agency for International Development). 2013. *Securing Vision 2030: Kenya Inclusive Growth Diagnostics*. Washington, DC: USAID.

World Bank. 2010. *Financing Higher Education in Africa*. Washington, DC: World Bank.

———. 2012. *Kenya Economic Update*. Washington, DC: World Bank.

———. 2013a. *Achieving Shared Prosperity in Kenya*. Washington, DC: World Bank.

———. 2013b. *Jobs for Shared Prosperity: Time for Action in Middle East and North Africa.* Washington, DC: World Bank.

———. 2014a. *Country Partnership Strategy for Kenya Draft.* Mimeo. Washington, DC: World Bank.

———. 2014b. *Kenya: A Supply Side Analysis of Skills for the Textile Sector.* Mimeo. Washington, DC: World Bank.

———. 2014c. *Student Financing for Tertiary Education in Kenya.* Mimeo. Washington, DC: World Bank.

———. 2014d. *Tertiary Education in Kenya.* Mimeo. Washington, DC: World Bank.

CHAPTER 3

Student Loans: A Tool for Equitable Expansion

Introduction

A scaled, well-functioning, effectively targeted, sufficiently endowed and financially sustainable student aid system will be necessary to support Kenya's ambitions for an expanded, quality post-secondary education system. In order for Kenya to fully capitalize on the significant human capital formation achieved through investments in improved primary and secondary education, the country will have to address the severe bottleneck developing at the post-secondary level due to the increasingly large cohorts of secondary graduates seeking entry to post-secondary education. In so doing, the country will need to ensure equitable access to vocational and higher education. This policy note addresses the specific policy challenges arising due to the need to provide student financing in support of equitable tertiary education expansion, and outlines the components necessary to ensure a successful system for student financing. The note presents an overview of the post-secondary education system in Kenya and analyzes challenges faced by, and opportunities to improve, the student financing system managed by Higher Education Loans Board (HELB) across three dimensions, and corresponding sections:

- Financial sustainability;
- The system's ability to effectively target students most in need; and
- Effective loan recovery.

Policy recommendations are provided for each section.

Context

With a population of 44 million and GDP per capita of US$1,260, Kenya has achieved middle-income country status; however 40 percent of the population continues to live below the national poverty line.[1] The country is heavily dependent on human capital formation for economic growth, and the government of Kenya (GoK)'s Vision 2030 places significant emphasis on the need to strengthen the education sector. At present, 26 million Kenyans are below the age of 25 years, equivalent to more than half of the country's population. The proportion of the population below the age of 25 is projected to rise to two thirds of a total population of 63 million by 2030 (World Bank 2014), with a majority of the labor force to be concentrated in urban areas. Moreover, the size of Kenya's labor force is projected to double by 2045 (World Bank 2013). Of the 25 million Kenyans above the age of 15, approximately 13 million have completed primary education and a further 7 million have completed a full cycle of secondary education. In order to ensure that the post-secondary education system has sufficient capacity to absorb the "tsunami" of youth graduating from secondary school, and that the country can fully capitalize on the associated demographic pay-off, there is a pressing need for to expand the Kenyan post-secondary education system.

If Kenya is to achieve its ambitions for economic transformation it will require the development of a stronger productive sector, improve the supply of skills and knowledge to the economy, and the development of strong regional partnerships. The country stands to accrue significant economic benefits through the application of quality skills and knowledge, and improved supply thereof, to key economic sectors such as agricultural and natural resources, and in the progressive development of the country's light manufacturing and information and communications technology (ICT) industries.

The Post-secondary Education Sector in Kenya

The development of post-secondary education in Kenya has entered a new phase, the relative success of which will critically impact the livelihoods of a growing youth population. The GOK has recently adopted an appropriate and well-defined post-secondary education policy framework aimed at addressing challenges associated with rapidly expanding enrollment. Recent developments in Kenya paint a picture of expanding student mobility programs as well as a rapidly growing higher education system that is nevertheless struggling to keep up with increasing demand for post-secondary places.

The country is facing a "Youth Tsunami" as students who entered the system following the introduction of free primary and secondary education begin to transition into post-secondary education. As shown in figure 3.1, the number of students taking the KCSE exam for admission to university is expected to increase from 543,403 in 2015 to 784,432 in 2016, equivalent to a year-on-year increase of 44.4 percent.

Higher education in Kenya has witnessed exponential growth, from one university (The University of Nairobi) to 22 chartered public universities (15 of which were established in 2012 and 2013), nine public university colleges, 17 private universities, five private university colleges, 11 universities operating under Letters of Interim Authority (LIA), and two registered universities.

Figure 3.1 Projections for Rise in Number of Students Transitioning from Secondary to Post-Secondary Education

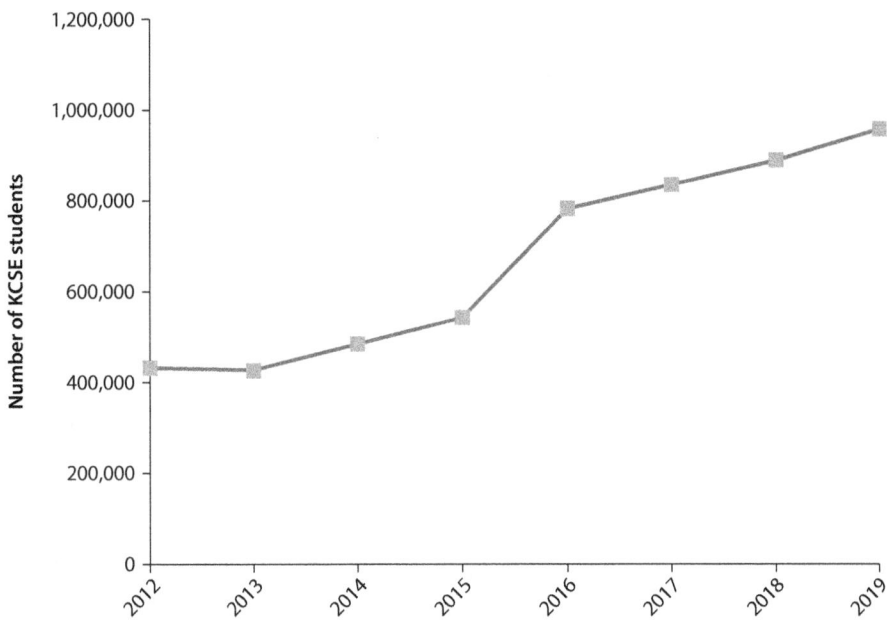

Source: Author's analysis of data from Kenya Bureau of Statistics.
Note: KCSE = Kenya Certificate of Secondary Education.

Kenya's post-secondary GER in 2009 was 4 percent[2] compared to a GER of 8 percent for SSA as a whole, and an average of 23 percent for lower-middle-income countries.[3] Comparatively poor rates of enrollment are a consequence of both demand and supply constraints. However, a critical challenge inhibiting further post-secondary enrollment relates to insufficient student financing in support of further education. KCSE graduates are required to obtain a passing grade of C+ or above to qualify for direct admission to university. In 2012, of the 123,000 students who achieved the C+ KCSE grade (or above), 53,000 enrolled in public universities, approximately 20,000 were admitted to the private universities, and a further 10,000 were admitted in the technical institutions. As a consequence approximately 40,000 qualifying young Kenyans were left with little hope of advancing their education beyond the secondary school level. Notwithstanding these concerning limitations, university enrollment in Kenya increased threefold between 2006 and 2012. Moreover, technical and vocational education and training (TVET) enrollment is increasing substantially, although the share of TVET enrollment as a proportion of total post-secondary enrollment has fallen from 47 percent in 2005 to 31 percent in 2013 (see figure 2.1). However, figure 2.1 only illustrates data for TVET institutes managed by the Ministry of Education, Science and Technology (MoEST). Several private companies provide industry-based training (for example, Toyota, housing financing, and Transcentury) and are seeking funding from HELB. A recent report entitled "Youth Employment Initiatives in Kenya" cited more than 1,000 TVET providers in Kenya, which may imply that the number of students enrolled in TVET education is substantially higher than what is captured in figure 2.1. The addition of enrollment from non-MoEST TVET education providers and other private institutions could increase TVET enrollment by a magnitude of three or four.

In SSA the returns to higher education are highest relative all other cycles of education; but so too is the cost of higher education. According to Montenegro and Patrinos (2014), average returns to tertiary education in SSA were 21.0 compared to 10.6 for secondary education, against worldwide returns of 14.6 to tertiary education. If capacity constraints force students to drop out of the education system before entering tertiary education, Kenya will forgo potentially significant developmental dividends associated with successful reforms in the primary and secondary education sectors.

In the absence of measures to ensure participation on the part of comparatively poor students, the significant costs associated with higher education can result in an inequitable distribution of benefits associated with tertiary education. While returns to education are highest for tertiary education, so is the cost of education. There is an absence of accurate contemporary household data to accurately assess equity considerations relative to the cost and affordability of tertiary education in Kenya. However, Murakami and Blom (2008) have demonstrated that the cost of tertiary education in Latin America can be as high as the equivalent of 60 percent of per-capita income per student, per year. Research by Hamadeh and Khoueiri (2010) demonstrates that tertiary enrollment decisions on the part of poor households are particularly sensitive to variations in price. The cost of tertiary education constitutes a significant barrier to entry for poor citizens, with the potential to deprive poorer students of access to the largest benefits associated with a single cycle of education.

Why Student Loans?

Given the financial considerations constraining access to tertiary education, who should foot the bill for tertiary education? This section of the policy note provides a rationale for cost-sharing in tertiary education, followed by a motivation for the provision of student loans as the basis of a cost-sharing mechanism, and finally, a rationale for publicly financed loans.

Rationale behind Cost-Sharing

Given the high unit costs associated with tertiary education relative to primary and secondary education, a policy extending universal access to free tertiary education would be extremely costly to governments and taxpayers. A rationale for cost-sharing is premised on the following arguments:

- Equity—if individuals benefit from education, they should contribute towards paying for it;

- Efficiency—when students pay for education they are more likely to be better consumers and institutions are more likely to be better service providers;
- Responsiveness—institutions that charge students for their education are more likely to align education provided with the needs of the market.

The Rationale for Student Loans

Student financing is a critical tool contributing towards efforts to ensure financial sustainability and equity in the context of an expanding tertiary education sector. Increasing the proportion of costs serviced by students through loans, reduces the dependence of the system on public financing as the system expands. Contingently, effectively targeted student financing mechanisms can promote equitable access to higher education (see figure 3.2). Loans can take a number of forms, with variations structured by terms of repayment, differential interest rates and collateral conditions. At the tertiary level the promotion of equity can be achieved through income-contingent student loans that cover university fees. Notwithstanding the mechanisms through which loans are structured, the terms of loan repayment (*inter alia*, interest rates charged, income thresholds for repayment, and the terms and rates of repayment) should be carefully considered.

Effective student loan systems in support of post-secondary education have been shown to reduce the rates at which students drop out of the sector. In Chile, dropout rates among CAE (Programa de Crédito con Aval del Estado) borrowers are one third of the dropout rate for students without CAE loans.[4] Some of the difference in dropout rates may be due to the additional scrutiny

Figure 3.2 Rationale for Student Loans

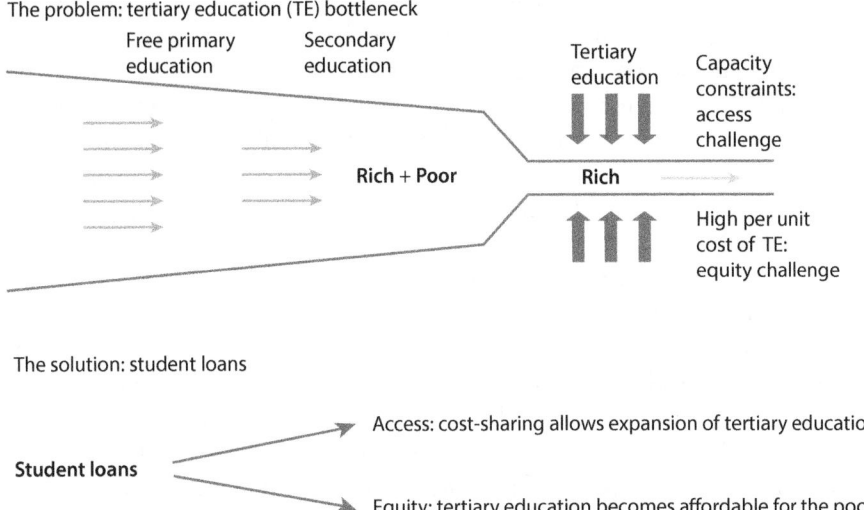

given to prospective CAE borrowers through the admissions process. However, the majority of the differential is likely to accrue to the program achieving its core mandate: making it easier for comparatively needy students to pay for their education, and allowing loan beneficiaries to concentrate on their studies without having to take on significant commitments to supplement their income. Evidence of lower dropout rates among CAE borrowers in Chile is consistent with evidence from other countries which suggest that student loans improve graduation rates. The efficiency savings accruing to a reduction in rates of dropout in tertiary education are considerable. Perhaps most importantly, a reduction in dropout rates improves the number of comparatively needy students graduating into productive livelihoods, and reduces the number of students who leave tertiary education disillusioned and without the degree or skills to which they aspired.

Rationale behind Public Financing
There is a strong rationale informing the imperative for public support to finance student loans. No large scale system for the provision of student loans can exist without public subsidy. This is due to the nature of loans in support of education which differ from commercial loans, such as mortgages and auto loans, due to the fact that investments in education constitute large sunk costs which cannot be re-possessed and sold to defray costs associated with loan delinquency. As a result commercial lenders rarely provide market-based long-term loans to support the costs of education.

Student loans are generally managed by a government agency, with a share of activities outsourced to service providers, even in middle and high-income countries including Canada, the U.K., and the United States. While there are cases of private financing for student loans, many of these examples have faced serious implementation challenges. In Chile private banks are assigned responsibility for originating and servicing loans through a "market-based" mechanism for allocating ownership of loan portfolios. While these innovations have been generally positive, especially in their intent, they incorporate some perverse incentives which generate additional costs. The Chilean system permits banks to accrue a relatively risk-free, profitable portfolio of loans, while charging inflated premiums and leaving high costs segments of the loan portfolio for servicing by Government.

In recent years, new systems of loan provision have been developed. For-profit private agencies in the US, as well as a number of non-profit institutions in developing countries, such as EDUCREDITO in Republica Bolivariana de Venezuela, are providing student loans. In Colombia, COLFUTURO was created as a foundation with capital contributions from both the public and private sectors in the early 1990s with the purpose of offering loans for students pursuing studies abroad in areas identified as being in the national interest. In Bangladesh, the Grameen Bank offers a student loan program for the children of poor families who are already the beneficiaries of small loans for productive activities.

However, most of these schemes are unable to provide loans on a national scale without complementary public finance.

Student Loans in Kenya

The Kenyan Higher Education Loans Board (HELB) was established as a State Corporation in July 1995 through an Act of Parliament (HELB Act Cap 213A), and is mandated to manage financial assistance for students enrolled in Kenyan public and private universities, and TVET institutes (see box 3.1). HELB has strong linkages between the Board of Directors and the management team, through the subcommittees of the board of directors. The intention of these linkages is to ensure that the Board delivers on its responsibilities. These committees include the Loans Disbursement and Recovery Committee; the Finance, Staff and General Purpose Committee; and the Procurement, Audit and Human Resources Committee. All committees are chaired by a member of the Board, and each committee's membership includes the Chief Executive Officer.

The following sections provide a detailed description of the key challenges faced by HELB, and contingent policy recommendation towards (a) ensuring financial sustainability; (b) improving the targeting of students in need; and (c) ensuring effective loan recovery mechanisms.

Box 3.1 HELB Loans at a Glance

Loans for Direct Entry Students (DES)
DES loans are targeted to students admitted to public or private universities within the EastAfrican Community. Students are identified following their graduation from high school through the Joint Admissions Board (JAB) or as self-sponsored students. Loans dispensed range between a minimum of 35,000 KSh and a maximum of 60,000 KSh, according to the student's need. Loans are subject to an interest rate of 4 percent per annum, and students are required to commence repayment of their loans on completion of their studies. Undergraduate loan repayment commences within one year of the completion of studies.

Alternative Loans (for Salaried Students)
Alternative loans are available for Postgraduate (Masters & PhD) and Undergraduate applicants who have salaried employment. Beneficiaries are able to repay their loans while studying, allowing the Board to generate income from application fees and interest charged to build and maintain a sustainable revolving fund. Loans are evaluated and awarded on the basis of the creditor's ability to pay while studying, and are subject to an interest rate of 12 percent per annum, repayable over 48 months.

Awards (per year)   PhD-Ksh: 60,000–200,000
                          Masters-Ksh: 60,000–200,000
                          CE-Ksh: 60,000–100,000

Challenge 1: Meeting Demand for Loans

HELB is facing unprecedented pressure due the anticipated increase in demand for loans which will accompany the "Tsunami" of students aspiring to enter the post-secondary education system from 2016. At present HELB is unable to dispense loans to meet the current levels of demand, and each year the gap between the demand for funds and HELB resources is expected to increase dramatically. In a context further characterized by rising tuition fees and weak loan recovery mechanisms, further financing gaps are expected to develop in the absence of rectifying interventions.

The greatest challenge to HELB is to resolve the financing gap between the demand for student loans and the availability of financial resources. The data presented below provides an overview of contemporary financial challenges faced by HELB:

- In 2012/2013, HELB disbursed loans to 118,426 students to a value of KSh 5.0 billion (US$45.4 million), against a total university student population of 380,000, representing coverage of 31.2 percent.
- The projected value of student loans disbursed in 2013/14 was KSh 7.3 billion (US$65 million). Government's contribution to HELB in 2013/14 was KSh 2.37 billion (US$21 million) against requested funding of KSh 14.5 billion (US$129 million). Loan recovery in 2013–14 amounted to KSh 2.54 billion (US$22.6 million), resulting in a funding gap of KSh 2.58 billion (US$23 million).
- In 2014 the funding environment became more challenging for HELB, and the financing gap widened further. Total loan applications grew by just over a third, from 53,000 in 2013 to 72,000 in 2014, inclusive of approximately 56,000 government-sponsored freshmen and 11,000 students admitted to TVET institutions. In 2014, HELB was allocated KSh 4 billion from the national budget, with loan recovery contributing KSh 3.3 billion. Total revenue of KSh 7.3 billion in 2014 represented half of the KSh 14.3 billion HELB needed to meet total demand. Serious delays in the disbursement of loans resulted in several students having to rely on their parents for tuition and living expenses to support off-campus accommodation.
- Misalignment of the admission and loan cycles added to financial challenges in 2014. Loan applicants who sat the KCSE exams in 2013 were admitted under the State's accelerated intake program, resulting in a surge of admissions which severely strained HELB's resources. Ordinarily, students enter the university system following a lag of one year. Frustration regarding access to finance, and the pace of loan disbursement led to strikes and unrest across the country, and protests at several universities including University of Nairobi, Kenyatta University, Jomo Kenyatta University of Agriculture and Technology (JKUAT), Masinde Muliro University of Science and Technology, Technical University of Mombasa, Dedan Kimathi, Meru and Karatina.

In order to estimate future demand for HELB loans, the core team calculated projections for 2014–2022 premised on secondary school enrollment (see table 3.1). The HELB team also conducted similar analysis; however there are key differences in underlying assumptions that resulted in a projected financing requirement of KSh 22 billion in 2022.

In an effort to assist HELB in accessing the required funding to service the expected "tsunami" of students, the current Board's strategic plan 2013–2018 incorporates several strategies to compliment GOK allocations. Key activities include: (a) seeking alternative sources of financing from the private sector and development partners, (b) outsourcing of loans recovery, and (c) the strengthening of ICT systems to improve data management and tracking.

Policy Recommendations

Given the magnitude of current gaps in financing to support loans for postsecondary education, and evidence that these gaps will continue to grow, there is an urgent to improve the flow of investments to HELB to sustainably meet projected demand. HELB will require significant financial support to cope with increasing demand for tertiary education. Moreover, in order for HELB to ensure

Table 3.1 Projections for HELB Funding Needs (All Figures in KSh)

Year	No. of KCSE students	Total no. of university students funded	Total student loans for higher education	Total no. of TVET students	Total student loans for TVET	Total funding requirement
2013	427,820	118,426	5,006,517,510	20,238	100,000,000	5,106,517,510
2014	485,089	143,588	6,475,716,658	100,000	2,000,000,000	8,475,716,658
2015	543,403	164,524	7,349,777,134	110,000	2,200,000,000	9,549,777,134
2016	783,432	199,829	8,860,369,581	121,000	2,420,000,000	11,280,369,581
2017	836,144	224,907	9,985,505,881	133,100	2,662,000,000	12,647,505,881
2018	890,542	262,226	11,668,219,122	146,410	2,928,200,000	14,596,419,122
2019	959,342	298,943	13,319,912,231	161,051	3,221,020,000	16,540,932,231
2020	964,000	330,898	14,769,290,433	177,156	3,543,122,000	18,312,412,433
2021	1,026,646	366,791	16,382,862,296	194,872	3,897,434,200	20,280,296,496
2022	1,118,902	401,175	17,919,011,244	214,359	4,287,177,620	**22,206,188,864**

Notes and assumptions:
- 2013 numbers are based on actual data; figures for 2014–2022 are projected based on secondary school enrollment.
- Calculations are based on transition rates derived from historic data and assume that historical precedent will continue unhindered:
  - Secondary Form 4 to KCSE: 93%;
  - KCSE to KCSE C+: 27%;
  - Eligible students (KCSE C+ and above) for admission to university: 30%. The government's calculations assume that this rate will increase by 25 basis points each year as a consequence of quality improvements. Given the lack of evidence of concrete policy interventions to motivate these improvements, this increase was not incorporated in the calculations above.
- For first-time students, the calculations assume:
  - 70% of admitted students are funded by HELB under JAB; and
  - Self-financed students increase by 10% each year commencing in 2013.
- A drop-out rate of 20% for continuing students in each year;
- Average loans KSh 39,500 for each first-year student, and average loans of KSh 43,500 for continuing students. These loan projections are consistent estimates provided by the government for 2013 loans and have been adjusted for projected inflation in each subsequent year. The government's calculations were based on an average loan of KSh 150,000. Given absence of reliable data with regard to tuition fees under the differentiated unit cost model, the calculations above assume consistent policies and do not incorporate a significant increase in fees.
- HELB = Higher Education Loan Board; KCSE = Kenya Certificate of Secondary Education; KSh Kenyan shillings; TVET = technical and vocational education and training.

its financial sustainability, it will need to focus on effective cost-recovery and improve its mechanisms for targeting beneficiaries. Recommendations in support of these ends include the following:

HELB mission. At present HELB's mission is to provide a "loan for every Kenyan." The government should consider revising the mission to focus loan provision towards needy students. (Detailed recommendations for improved targeting of beneficiaries are provided in Section 5.1). Changing the mission of the HELB would also assist in managing expectations with regard to the availability of loans. Students who are able to pay their tuition fees should not feel entitled to loans that could be better utilized by poor students.

HELB should focus on seeking alternate sources of funding by delegating fund management to, *inter alia*, local governments and private companies. Initiatives similar to the Afya Elimu Fund, a public private partnership between HELB, USAID, the Kenya Private Sector Alliance and selected government ministries, are critical for establishing sustainable alternative sources of financing in support of higher education. HELB has commenced a process to consolidate unclaimed assets (lottery wins, mobile credit, etc.), however the allocation of these funds to HELB will require strong political support. HELB has also recently signed a Memorandum of Understanding (MOU) for TVET training under the one million artisans program with the Housing Finance Foundation (HFF). Similar initiatives should be initiated, strengthened and supported to sustain student financing for relevant post-secondary education of a high quality.

Focus on science, technology, engineering, and mathematics (STEM). The process to align university fees with the differentiated unit costs of programs are expected to exert upward pressure on fees, specifically in programs relating to science and technology. In order to ensure that enrollment in STEM programs is not compromised in the face of increased costs, student-financing will need to be strengthened, and should integrate specific mechanisms to encourage enrollment in STEM fields.

Lowering administrative costs. According to HELB's 2012 Annual Report operational expenses accounted for approximately 22 percent of total expenses (KSh 143,257,733 operating costs of KSh 636,261,111 in total expenses). HELB should work to reduce these costs by outsourcing targeting and recovery operations, and through improving efficiency in its day-to-day operations (details on outsourcing recovery are provided in Section 6.1).

The role of universities and the private sector in sustaining financing. Universities can play a critical role in promoting financial literacy, and in helping to shoulder the burden of student loans. Tertiary education institutions directly benefit from student loans, due to the fact that loans increase the number of students who can afford to pay for further education. The following recommendations are closely linked to proposed interventions for HELB:

- Universities should take responsibility for student loan payments during a student's period of study. The Government should consider requiring

universities to take responsibility for students who drop out and for underperforming students admitted with student loans. The financial risk of students dropping out is primarily an academic risk, which universities should mitigate through rigorous admissions criteria and the provision of high quality teaching, including remedial programs to improve completion rates.
- Tertiary institutions should be encouraged to guarantee a percentage of the value of loans, since low dropout and default rates would mean that new revenues would exceed costs. If managed effectively, tertiary institutions would benefit from the implementation of these measures.

Challenge 2: Targeting

Even in a context in which government allocations to HELB are increased, demand for student loans is likely to continue to exceed available financing. As a consequence there will be an added impetus to target assistance to the most needy students.

In the 2013/2014 fiscal year 58,213 new students applied for loans in support of undergraduate studies, of which 52,950 students were awarded loans ranging in value from KSh 35,000 to KSh 60,000. The average loan awarded by HELB was to the value of KSh 41,450 per student, and 69 percent of students received a loan of KSh 37,000 for the first year of their undergraduate studies. The determination of loans for each student is premised on a Means Testing Instrument (MTI), which evaluates each applicant against a set of criteria designed to assess relative need and the government's priorities. The MTI is critical for ensuring equitable access to post-secondary education, and its effective implementation is a key priority for government. The specific MTI instrument varies slightly by type of loan product, but all models score students across a range of indicators to establish relative need. These indicators include, *inter alia*, household income, gender, number of siblings, and a determination of who paid for the secondary education.

Analysis of 2013 data for loan applicants and recipients demonstrates a significant gap between the average income of loan applicants and recipients, implying that the MTI is effective in identifying students with the greatest needs. Household income for all loan applicants in 2013/2014 averaged KSh 169,585 (US$1,935), while the average household income of loan recipients was KSh 74,997 (US$856). GDP per capita in 2012 was US$1,260, underscoring the effectiveness of MTI in targeting comparatively poor students (see table 3.2).

Table 3.2 Average Household Income of Loan Applicants and Recipients in Comparison with GDP per Capita

GDP per capita (2014)	Loan applicants	Loan recipients
US$1,260	US$1,935	US$856

Although the MTI is demonstrably effective in identifying students in comparative need, it does not perform as well with regard to assigning loans in proportion to need. The MTI scorecard divides household income in five categories wherein households with the lowest income quintile earn less than KSh 20,000 per annum, and the highest earn KSh 150,000 per annum. The amount to be loaned to students varies according to the income of the household. The mean loan extended to students from the lowest income group is USD 504 compared to USD 436 for the highest income group is. In practice this means that the MTI determines an average loan for students in the lowest income group just 20 percent higher than those extended to students from the richest income group. When one considers that households in the wealthiest quintile accrue seven times more income than those in the lowest income group per year, a 20 percent differential in the average loan extended to these categories of students is relatively insignificant. Average loans by each income group are illustrated in figure 3.3.

A comparison of the distribution of income of loan applicants and recipients, with estimated household income from a 2013 representative household survey demonstrates inconsistencies between the distribution of average household income and Kenyan household income, implying that stronger mechanisms are required to verify reported income.[5] According to the household survey, 22.9 percent of Kenyans have an annual household income between KSh 12,000 and KSh 36,000 (see figure 3.4). Two points arising from the analysis are pertinent:

- The distribution of overall household income is skewed to the left, while the distribution of loan applicants peaks twice: with 27.9 percent falling in the lowest range of income (below KSh 12,000), 23 percent in the overall

Figure 3.3 Average Loans, by Income Group

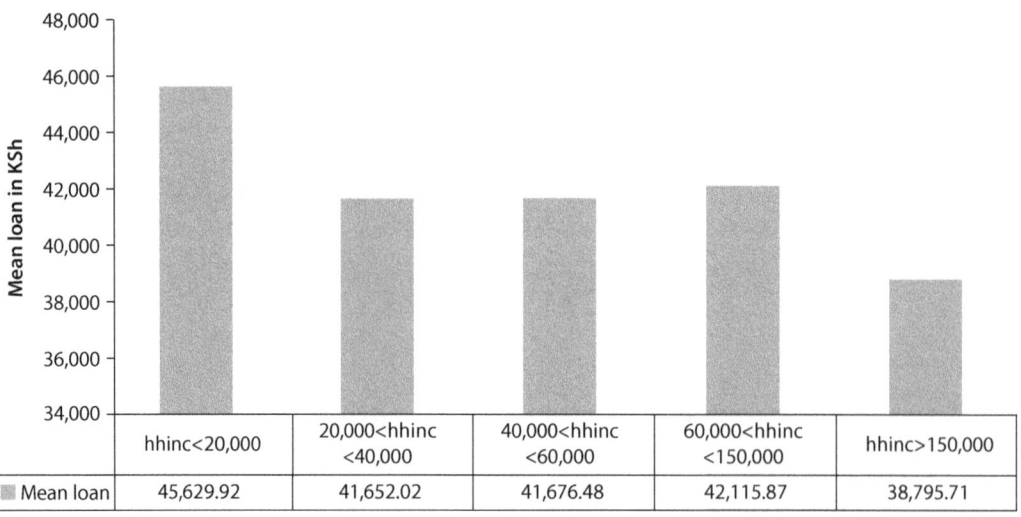

	hhinc<20,000	20,000<hhinc<40,000	40,000<hhinc<60,000	60,000<hhinc<150,000	hhinc>150,000
Mean loan	45,629.92	41,652.02	41,676.48	42,115.87	38,795.71

Note: hhinc = household income; KSh = Kenyan shillings.

Figure 3.4 Comparison of Household Incomes of Loan Applicants and Recipients to Average Households in Kenya

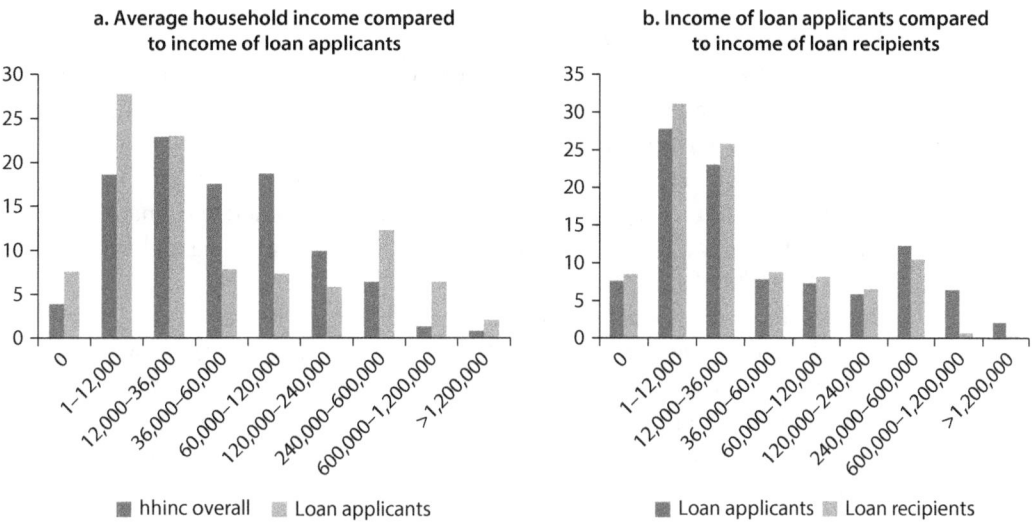

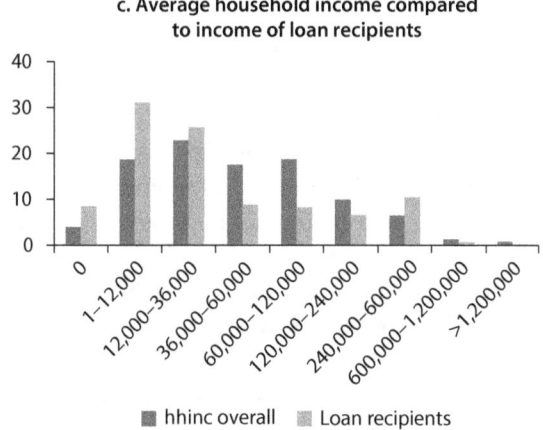

Note: hhinc = household income.

average range and 12.26 percent in a much higher range (KSh 240,000 to KSh 600,000). The distribution of household income for loan applicants does not match an expected distribution which one would expect to be skewed to the right (given that households that access post-secondary education are relatively well off compared to the population at large);
• The percentage of loan applicants reporting zero income is much higher than the equivalent group in the household survey.

These patterns may be indicative of a tendency among loan applicants to under-report household income, and underscores the need to strengthen income verification mechanisms. The distribution of household incomes among loan recipients mirrors that of the loan applicants.

Policy Recommendations

Transparent eligibility criteria are critical for ensuring that subsidies for student finance are extended to the most deserving students. HELB should strengthen linkages between student loan repayment practices and the possibility of beneficiaries obtaining future loans and financial assistance from the financial sector. Improving engagement with commercial banks and the financial sector will assist efforts towards establishing a system for maintaining and tracking the credit histories of students and guarantors.

Specific recommendations include the following:

HELB should maintain data on the verification process to track progress, and promote awareness of the system. The distribution of loan applicants' and recipients' household income against surveys of household income implies underreporting of income on the part of loan beneficiaries. HELB should consider incorporating structured mechanisms to verify data collected for the loan application scorecard, even if this is initially done on pilot basis.

The MTI scorecard is not sufficiently capable of accurately capturing variations in household incomes on the part of loan recipients. Further analysis of the weights assigned to each score indicator should be undertaken to refine the utility of the instrument, and further prioritize low-income students in the application process.

Targeting mechanisms should be made more predictable and transparent, complemented by public awareness campaigns. These measures will assist HELB in managing the expectations of applicants; encourage comparatively poor students to apply for assistance (see box 3.2); and erode the sense of entitlement among some students who can afford higher education, which has in some instances contributed to social unrest.

Box 3.2 Chilean Loan Scheme—A Focus on Equity

Chile's Programa de Crédito con Aval del Estado (CAE) has helped hundreds of thousands of qualified but financially needy Chileans access tertiary education. At present approximately 147,000 students with CAE assistance are enrolled in tertiary education, the majority of whom would not otherwise have been able to access higher education. A further 69,000 students who would likely have been able to support the costs of tertiary study are benefitting from CAE loans. Current CAE supported enrollment is likely to produce 151,000 graduates, three-quarters of whom would likely never have graduated without access to a CAE loan, and one-quarter would likely have graduated with significant economic hardship. Two-thirds of CAE beneficiaries are drawn from the lowest two quintiles of Chilean household income. Outcomes data demonstrates the profound role CAE is playing in transforming equity in Chilean tertiary education.

Challenge 3: Weak Recovery Mechanisms

The financial viability of a student loan scheme is dependent in part on the degree of interest rate subsidy, default rates, and administrative costs. The default rate, in turn, is a function of the income of the graduates, the effectiveness of collection mechanisms, and the type of repayment schedule applied (fixed payments versus graduated payments and length of the grace period). In 2014, KSh 13 billion in loans disbursed to 144,040 loan beneficiaries had not matured, while a further 98,676 beneficiaries are servicing loans to the value of KSh 14.4 billion, translating to a performance rate of 60.7 percent. At present 76,221 HELB creditors with total loans valued at KSh 8.4 billion are considered delinquent; of these 31,879 are being actively pursued for loan repayment (see tables 3.3 and 3.4).

HELB has invested significantly in boosting the rates of loan recovery, resulting in an average increase in loan recovery of 15 percent per year from 56 million in the financial year 1995–96 to 3.2 billion in 2013–14. HELB has also devised new strategies to improve loan recovery in an effort to boost its fund by tracing past beneficiaries through employers and statutory bodies such as the Kenya Revenue Authority (KRA), the National Hospital Insurance Fund (NHIF), and the National Social Security Fund (NSSF).

Policy Recommendations

In order to ensure the sustainability of HELB's revolving fund, loan recovery systems should be further strengthened through the use of documentation and innovative methods to improve the timely repayment of disbursed loans. HELB is still a relatively young program, and deficiencies need to be addressed to mitigate the institutionalization of "culture of default". The following policy recommendations should be considered to achieve these ends.

Table 3.3 HELB Loan Recovery Status

PAR distribution	Loanees	KSh (m)
Records without ID	17,353	686
Loanees under grace period	26,989	3,910
Net PAR	31,879	3,894
Total PAR	76,221	8,490

Note: HELB - Higher Education Loan Board; ID = identification; KSh = Kenyan shillings; m = millions; PAR = portfolio at risk.

Table 3.4 Loan Book as of June 30, 2014

Disbursement		Performing		Portfolio at risk		Cleared		Un-mature	
Loanees	KSh (m)	Loanees	KSh (m)	Loanees	KSh (m)	Loanees	KSh (m)	Loanees	KSh (m)
430,680	46,845	99,986	14,431	76,221	8,490	92,782	8,743	161,691	14,880

Note: KSh = Kenyan shillings; m = millions.

Improve efficient collection mechanisms to minimize default, including an appropriate legal framework. HELB currently issues HELB clearance certificates which are required for processing employment and immigration documents. However, the private sector has only partially bought into requiring a clearance certificate as a pre-requisite for employment. Furthermore, there are poor mechanisms for ensuring compliance for professionals, such as lawyers and doctors, in private practice.

Assess the feasibility of requiring a co-guarantor for loans. The practice of not requiring the down payment of collateral should be continued, however HELB should assess the impact of requiring an adult co-guarantor to encourage greater accountability through the loan application process. The introduction of a co-guarantor requirement may result in a short-term decline in applications, but it is likely that it will improve loan repayment practices in the medium- to long-term.

Improve reporting and analysis of loan portfolios and recovery trends. HELB should ensure that it captures data across various categories of institutions and student characteristics; including, *inter alia*, levels of education, grades, socioeconomic background, region and program of study. Establish mechanisms for assessing the share of graduates from institutions of higher education engaged in informal employment, and tailor recovery mechanisms to improve loan recovery from this sub-set of beneficiaries.

Investment in ICT. Investment will not only help to facilitate the improved recovery of loans but, moreover, contribute to the establishment of sustainable mechanisms for tracking students through the repayment cycle.

Outsourcing. Several student loan schemes in the US and Canada have successfully outsourced aspects of the loan process; including, *inter alia*, administration, database management, loan disbursement and loan recovery. HELB has recently commenced the outsourcing of loan recovery to individual agents, but the program would benefit from the scaling up of these activities and the linking of successful loan recovery and verification to performance-based incentives.

Improve engagement with students. Students often take on student debt without a clear understanding of the terms of their loan, or consequences of default, leading to instances of confusion regarding the terms of repayment and interest rates. Higher education institutions should be required to provide loan counseling to students upon admission to the institution and their graduation. Students should be encouraged to repay their HELB loans in a timely manner to improve the likelihood of receiving other loans and financial assistance in the future. These efforts should be complemented by an information and marketing campaign to promote knowledge of the student loan program to improve awareness of the program among eligible students and institutions.

Risk sharing with private institutions and families:

- Private institutions accrue substantial benefits from financial resources derived from HELB supported students, and play an important role in educating graduates in a number of critical professions. HELB should explore requiring private institutions to take co-responsibility, in the form of a partial guarantee or an upfront co-payment, to offset risks associated with loan default (as is the case in Chile and Colombia).

- Families, especially affluent families, reduce their out-of-pocket expenditure through access to student loans. Introducing a requirement for parents, the extended family, or community to partially, or fully, guarantee loan repayment would improve accountability with regard to loan repayment, reduce government costs, and further incentivize academic performance on the part of students.

Increase the involvement of universities and institutions in the management of student loans. The use of institutional loan recovery rates as determinant factors informing future loan allocations will incentivize universities to improve loan repayment on the part of their students. HELB would benefit from support extended by institutions as universities and colleges can more easily access students to provide advice on financial support programs. Moreover, the provision of institutional support and mentoring programs would help to facilitate improved retention, academic performance and rates of graduation with concurrent positive effects for the student loan cycle.

Notes

1. Source: World Bank Country Profile—Kenya, 2013; Ministry of Finance, 2014.
2. World Bank Data—Country Profile Kenya; there is no updated number on overall GER.
3. 2012 World Development Indicators table 2.11.
4. Chile's State Guaranteed Student Loan Program Report 2011.
5. FinAccess National Survey 2013: This survey is based on the responses of 6,449 individuals from 710 clusters (12 households per cluster) to accurate national, regional and urbanization (urban/rural) sampling. The North Eastern region was omitted from the survey due to security concerns. The ideal comparator group would be drawn from a sample of households with students enrolled in post-secondary education. Unfortunately, these data were not available but should be collected for future analysis.

References

Hamadeh, M., and R. Khoueiri. 2010. "Demand Elasticities for Higher Education in the United States." *International Journal of Business and Economics Perspective* 5 (2): 60–67.

Montenegro, Claudio E., and Harry Anthony Patrinos. 2014. "Comparable Estimates of Returns to Schooling around the World." Policy Research Working Paper WPS 7020, World Bank, Washington, DC.

Murakami, Y., and A. Blom. 2008. "Accessibility and Affordability of Tertiary Education in Brazil, Colombia, Mexico and Peru within a Global Context." Policy Research Working Paper 4517, World Bank, Washington, DC.

World Bank. 2013a. *Achieving Shared Prosperity in Kenya*. Washington, DC: World Bank.

———. 2013b. *Jobs for Shared Prosperity: Time for Action in Middle East and North Africa*. Washington, DC: World Bank.

———. 2014a. *Country Partnership Strategy for Kenya Draft*. Mimeo. Washington, DC: World Bank.

———. 2014b. *Kenya: A Supply Side Analysis of Skills for the Textile Sector*. Mimeo. Washington, DC: World Bank.

———. 2014c. *Student Financing for Tertiary Education in Kenya*. Mimeo. Washington, DC: World Bank.

———. 2014d. *Tertiary Education in Kenya*. Mimeo. Washington, DC: World Bank.

CHAPTER 4

Governance of Post-Secondary Education in Kenya

Introduction

This policy note will outline governance of post-secondary education in Kenya, with a focus on changes in governance structures necessitated by the passing of the new Kenyan Constitution (2010) and contingent Acts. For the purpose of focused analysis, this note will concentrate on the higher education sector, noting that the technical and vocational education and training (TVET) sector is undergoing an equivalent transformation of governance structures. Analysis will be guided by the need to answer two primary questions:

1. How will reforms being implemented in Kenya's higher education sector impact the governance and management of the higher education system in Kenya?
2. What challenges arise through the process of reform implementation with regard to institutional governance and management of the sector?

Governance is understood to be a system of structures and processes informing decision-making. Reforming governance practices may require the creation of new structures. Structures are usually understood to relate to offices, positions, formal roles, and committees within an organization, institution or system. The term management is used to imply the implementation of decisions involving specified criteria for the allocation of resources in support of various activities; the delegation of tasks to specific groups; and the evaluation of performance. This note will focus on: (a) the rationale for reform in the Kenyan context; (b) the legal and institutional framework structuring higher education in Kenya, with a specific focus on the implications of the Universities Act (2012) and new governance structures and institutions established by the Act; (c) the governance and management of institutions, including a focus on the basis of autonomy for universities and the appointment of university leadership; (d) the management of systems for accreditation and quality assurance in the higher education sector; and

(e) the management of the private higher education subsector in Kenya. The note includes a discussion of contingent reforms in the TVET sector, and concludes with an analysis of the implications of reform and a set of policy recommendations.

The National Vision: The Context of Reforms in Higher Education

The Kenya Vision 2030 (Republic of Kenya 2007), which states as its aim the intention to transform Kenya into a "newly industrializing, middle income, globally competitive and prosperous country," and the new Constitution of Kenya frame the basis for reform in all sectors in Kenya, including higher education. In this context, and in order to build on earlier reforms, the Ministry for Higher Education, Science and Technology (MoEST) established a Taskforce on the Alignment of the Higher Education, Science and Technology Sector with the Constitution of Kenya (Republic of Kenya 2012a, and the Policy Framework for Education and Training On Reforming Education and Training Sectors in Kenya (Republic of Kenya 2012b). The output of the taskforce, and contingent documents, specify a new legal framework for the management and governance of higher education in Kenya. Binding legislation on the sector includes:

- The Universities Act, 2012 (Republic of Kenya 2012c)
- The Technical and Vocational Education and Training Act, 2013 (Republic of Kenya 2013a)
- The Science, Technology and Innovation Act, 2013 (Republic of Kenya 2013b).

This note will focus on the implications of the first two pieces of legislation.

In contrast to the constitution it replaced, The Constitution of Kenya (2010) recognizes and promotes provisions with regard to education, youth, and the promotion of science and technology. The new Constitution directly impacts the governance and management of higher education, science and technology through provisions relating to, *inter alia*, freedom of expression, inclusive of rights relating to academic freedom and freedom of scientific research; the right to education as a universally applied socio-economic right; the right for persons with disability to access educational institutions and facilities; and rights to opportunity for minority and marginalized groups.

The new legal framework for higher education necessitated by Vision 2030 and the 2010 Constitution is articulated in the Universities Act of 2012. The Act states as its aim the need to "invest in the people of Kenya" through the provision of globally competitive and quality education, training, and research in support of national development. Vision 2030, *inter alia*, called for the intensified application of science, technology and innovation to raise productivity and efficiency in Kenya's economic, social and the political sectors, which serve as the three organizing "pillars" of the 2030 Vision.

The Universities Act frames a context in which the national values and principals of governance as articulated by the new Constitution guide higher education institutions in the discharging of their functions and powers. In this regard, Clause 2 of the Act, drawing on Article 10 of the Constitution, requires institutions to, *inter alia*, promote the quality and relevance of programs delivered; enhance equity and accessibility in the delivery of education services; promote inclusive, efficient, effective and transparent systems and practices of governance, and maintain public trust; ensure sustainability and the adoption of management best-practices and institutionalize systems of checks and balances; promote private-public partnerships in the service of university education and development; and institutionalize non-discriminatory practices.

The Higher Education Legal and Institutional Framework

Capitalizing on increasing demand for higher education in Kenya will play a critical role in the achievement of Vision 2030 and the ideals of the Constitution. Kenya's higher education system is becoming more complex due to its growth and the increasing sophistication of public and private institutions, the need for the system and the state to respond to the rapid internationalization of university education, and the more general trends informing a transition to an increasingly knowledge-based economy. Challenges with regard to managing these complexities are heightened by a context in which a significant expansion of, and improved completion rates in, primary and secondary education have resulted in surging demand for post-secondary education. These challenges are front and center as the government seeks to implement new governance structures, guided by new policies, strategies and legal regimes.

Kenya's public and private universities are divided into the following categories.[1]

- *Chartered Universities* are universities that have met the set standards for full university accreditation by the Commission for University Education (CUE). Charters are granted by the President on the recommendation of both the Cabinet Secretary responsible for education and the CUE.
- *Universities with Letter of Interim Authority (LIA)* are universities that have received a LIA issued by the Cabinet Secretary responsible for Education on the recommendation of the CUE. Prior to the passing of the 2012 Universities Act, in alignment with now repealed legislation, only private universities could be granted an LIA by the Commission for Higher Education (CHE). A university granted LIA status operates with close supervision and guidance from CUE while awaiting a Charter. LIA institutions are required to establish: a governing body; develop physical facilities; assemble academic resources; admit students; and establish internal quality assurance mechanisms towards achieving Charter status.
- *Registered Private Universities* are private universities established prior to the establishment of the CHE in 1985. Registered Private Universities are at

various stages of developing institutional resources and facilities towards full chartered accreditation.
- *Foreign universities*. The Universities Act 2012 makes provision for the registration of universities established outside Kenya that offer university education within the country. Foreign universities are subject to the same accreditation process as applied to Kenyan universities. A foreign university may enter into an arrangement with an existing institution in Kenya for the purposes of offering its programs or joint programs with the prior approval of the CUE.

University education in Kenya has witnessed exponential growth from one university (The University of Nairobi) in 1970, to 22 fully chartered public universities (15 of which were established in 2012 and 2013), nine public university colleges, 17 private universities, five private university colleges, 11 Universities with LIAs and two Registered Universities at the end of 2013 (see table 3.4 for details).

The passing of the Universities Act in 2012 led to the establishment of 12 new chartered public universities, through the upgrading of Constituent University Colleges at seven existing public universities to full university status. Moreover, enrollment at the original seven public universities has rapidly increased, especially on the part of privately sponsored students. The establishment of 12 new universities, initially as affiliates of existing universities, represented the culmination of a set of interventions implemented over the course of five years preceding the passing of the 2012 Act. These measures were initiated in response to the anticipated increase in pressure for university spaces from 2015 arising due to the successful expansion and reform of basic education, especially introduction of free primary education in 2003.

The number of students enrolled in Kenya's education system has increased substantially since the introduction of free primary and secondary education. Recent statistics (Kenya National Bureau of Statistics Facts and Figures 2013) demonstrate an increase in primary enrollment from 8,831,400 in 2009 to 9,997,900 in 2012, and a concurrent increase in secondary enrollment from 1,472,600 in 2009 to 1,914,800 in 2012 (see table 4.1). Improved primary and secondary school enrollment has led to significant growth in university enrollment, with at least 240,500 students enrolled in local private and public universities in 2012, from 177,700 in 2009, more than half of whom were enrolled in public universities with privately sponsorship. Box 4.1 captures data relating to the growth of university enrollment between 2009 and 2012 (CUE 2013).

Table 4.1 Student Enrollment in Public and Private Universities

	2009	2010	2011	2012
Enrollment in public and private universities	177,700	117,600	198,300	240,500

Source: Kenya National Bureau of Statistics: Kenya Facts and Figures 2013.

Box 4.1 Status of Universities in Kenya, 2014

Chartered Public Universities
1. University of Nairobi (1970)
2. Moi University (1984)
3. Kenyatta University (1985)
4. Egerton University (1987)
5. Jomo Kenyatta University of Agriculture and Technology (JKUAT)—(1994)
6. Maseno University (MSU)—(2001)
7. Masinde Muliro University of Science and Technology (2007)
8. Dedan Kimathi University of Technology (2012)
9. Chuka University (2013)
10. Technical University of Kenya (2013)
11. Technical University of Mombasa (2013)
12. Pwani University (2013)
13. Kisii University (2013)
14. University of Eldoret (2013)
15. Maasai Mara University (2013)
16. Jaramogi Oginga Odinga University of Science and Technology (2013)
17. Laikipia University (2013)
18. South Eastern Kenya University (2013)
19. Meru University of Science and Technology (2013)
20. Multimedia University of Kenya (2013)
21. University of Kabianga (2013)
22. Karatina University (2013)

Public University Constituent Colleges
1. Murang'a University College (JKUAT) (2011)
2. Machakos University College (KU) (2011)
3. The Co-operative University College of Kenya (JKUAT) (2011)
4. Embu University College (UoN) (2011)
5. Kirinyaga University College (KU) (2011)
6. Rongo University College (MU) (2011)
7. Kibabii Universtity College (MMUST) (2011)
8. Garissa University College (MU) (2011)
9. Taita Taveta University College (JKUAT) (2011)

Chartered Private Universities
1. University of Eastern Africa, Baraton (1991)
2. Catholic University of Eastern Africa (CUEA) (1992)
3. Scott Theological College (1992)
4. Daystar University (1994)
5. United States International University (1999)
6. Africa Nazarene University (2002)
7. Kenya Methodist University (2006)
8. St. Paul's University (2007)
9. Pan Africa Christian University (2008)
10. Strathmore University (2008)
11. Kabarak University (2008)
12. Mount Kenya University (2011)
13. Africa International University (2011)
14. Kenya Highlands Evangelical University (2011)
15. Great Lakes University of Kisumu (GLUK) (2012)
16. KCA University (2013)
17. Adventist University of Africa (2013)

Private University Constituent Colleges
1. Hekima University College (CUEA) (1993)
2. Tangaza University College (CUEA) (1997)
3. Marist International University College (CUEA) (2002)
4. Regina Pacis University College (CUEA) (2010)
5. Uzima University College (CUEA) (2012)

Universities with Letter of Interim Authority
1. Kiriri Women's University of Science and Technology (2002)
2. Aga Khan University (2002)
3. Gretsa University (2006)
4. Presbyterian University of East Africa (2008)
5. Inoorero University—2009
6. The East African University (2010)
7. GENCO University—2010
8. Management University of Africa (2011)
9. Riara University—2012
10. Pioneer International University (2012)
11. UMMA University (2013)

Registered Private Universities
1. Nairobi International School of Theology
2. East Africa School of Theology

Source: Commission for University Education.

Enrollment in universities is projected to further increase from 240,500 in 2013 to 970,00 by 2018 (CUE 2013), equivalent to a 303 percent increase in enrollment in five years, dubbed a "tsunami for higher education. The government will face significant challenges in facilitating increased access to university while maintaining the quality of higher education delivered. Newly established and older universities will concurrently need to upgrade their human resources and facilities to ensure students continue to receive quality training in an environment conducive to learning.

In addition to the expansion of the basic education, a number of additional factors are contributing to the unprecedented expansion and diversification of Kenya's higher education. Shifting demand in the labor market for increasingly sophisticated skills and competencies aligned to a modern, globally-competitive and increasingly knowledge-based economy and the need to ensure the continued upgrading of professional skills in response to economic change, buttressed by the tendency of professions to seek enhanced status through education, are additional factors informing rising demand for post-secondary education. Some of the universities established by the government in 2013 are deliberately intended to produce skilled workers for underserved sectors of the economy and regions of the country, and to contribute to improving equal access to tertiary education. These regions include the Coastal area of Kenya, where two new universities have been established[2] and northern Kenya,[3] where, in addition to addressing equity issues, there is an urgent need to supply skilled workers for the further development of regional clusters of industry (especially petroleum, gas and coal).

To ensure that the quality university education provision is not compromised, the sector must address a number of challenges arising as a consequence of growing demand for university education. A significant challenge in this regard entails the training and recruitment of sufficient numbers of qualified university staff to address existing deficits in teaching staff and accommodate the projected increase in enrollment. It is estimated that, at a minimum, 23,400 lecturers and other teaching staff will be needed by 2018 to service increased enrollment, off a current base of 6,200 teaching staff in universities (CUE). The GOK will need to develop and implement an extensive human resource development strategy to reduce lecturer to student ratios and guarantee the continued delivery of quality education.

The Universities Act, 2012

The Universities Act passed by Parliament in 2012 serves as the primary law governing higher education in Kenya. The general purpose of the Universities Act is to provide for the development and management of university education in Kenya, with a specific focus on:

- Outlining the role and powers of government in the sector, especially the relevant Ministry responsible for higher education;
- Provide for the establishment, accreditation and governance of universities;
- Provide for the establishment of key government agencies, or buffer bodies, for: the establishment, accreditation of higher education and quality assurance (the CUE as a successor to the CHE); co-ordination of the placement of government-sponsored students in universities and colleges (the Kenya Universities and Colleges Placement Service as the successor to the Joint

Admissions Board [JAB]); and the co-ordination of funding for public universities and the provision of conditional grants and loans to private universities, and overall coordination for the funding of universities (the Universities Funding Board);
- Outlining systems and practices for the governance and management of universities, including governing organs and the appointment of university officers; and
- Outlining financial duties and responsibilities, and an organizing rubric for universities.

The Universities Act repealed all the previous Acts associated with the establishment of Kenya's original seven public universities.[4] The 2012 Act also replaces the Act that established the CHE (the precursor of the CUE), which also served to govern the establishment, accreditation and management of private universities.[5] Prior to the passing of the Act public universities operated as self-regulating entities, while private universities were subject to detailed regulatory controls administered by the CHE. The Act has removed the duality that previously existed in the establishment of public and private universities, and in systems for ensuring quality assurance and management. The new Universities Act 2012 has served in part to consolidate legislation as it applied to both public and private universities, and is intended to subject the entire sector to one set of guiding legislation. The largest criticism relating quality and relevance in the public university system in the pre-2012 era related to the absence of external quality assurance mechanisms overseen by an independent agency. To this end, the new Act established and articulated the functions and role of the new CUE.

Commission for University Education (CUE)

Against this background, and established by the Universities Act, 2012, CUE is the successor to the CHE with the following functions:

- Promoting the objectives of university education;
- Advising the government on policy relating to university education;
- Promoting standards for university education;
- Monitoring and evaluation to ensure universities comply with standards and guidelines;
- Licensing of student recruitment agencies operating in Kenya and the activities of foreign universities;
- Developing admissions policies and requirements for universities; recognizing and equating degrees, diplomas and certificates conferred or awarded by foreign universities and institutions in accordance with the standards and guidelines articulated by the CUE;
- The collection, dissemination and maintenance of data relating to university education;
- Accreditation and regulation of university education in Kenya;

- The promotion of quality research and innovation; and
- Monitoring and evaluating of university education systems with respect to the promotion of national development goals.

The core functions of CUE mirror those of CHE, with the addition of accreditation and quality assurance, and quality enhancement, responsibilities applied to the public university subsector.

Kenya Universities and Colleges Central Placement Service (KUCCPS)

The Universities Act of 2012 established the Kenya Universities and Colleges Central Placement Service (KUCCPS) as a successor to the JAB. Under the previous regime, JAB coordinated the admission of government-sponsored students to public universities for over 20 years. The main aim of JAB was to ensure that only qualified candidates received priority admission to public universities with government sponsorship. While the function of JAB was not codified in law, it was acceded to by the Senates of all public universities which served as the legal organs overseeing admissions to public universities. JAB was chaired by the Vice Chancellors of the public universities on a rotational basis. JAB's mandate did not extend to the admission of students to private universities.

The main function of the newly created KUCCPS is to co-ordinate the placement of government-sponsored students in public and private universities and colleges. It is also responsible for disseminating information on university programs, their costs and the areas of study prioritized by the government. KUCCPS was officially inaugurated in February 2014 and managed the placement of government supported student for the 2014–15 academic years. Unlike JAB, which only admitted students to public universities, the new Placement Board may place government sponsored students in both public and private universities and colleges. KUCCPS is mandated to establish criteria to facilitate access on the part of student to programs for which they have applied, taking into account the students' qualifications and listed priorities. KUCCPS is responsible for the development of career programs for students and for collecting and retaining data relating to university and college placement.

In addition to the establishment of a centralized student admissions system, coordinated by KUCCPS, the Universities Act allows universities and colleges to independently admit students to its programs in accordance with approved admissions criteria. In this regard, existing arrangements at public universities for the admission of privately sponsored and full-fee paying students are expected to continue outside the aegis of KUCCPS. As such, the established dual admissions processes for government sponsored and privately sponsored students will continue in public universities.

The University Fund and the Funding Board

The Universities Fund, and the contingent Funding Board established to manage the fund, constitute critical new independent institutions established under the Universities Act. The Board will be responsible for advising the government in matters relating to the funding of university education, and related policy issues, and is responsible for the management of a fund to support the financing of universities. The fund's activities will not be limited to public universities, but allow of the extension of conditional grants and loans to private universities. The Board is mandated to establish the maximum differential unit cost for academic programs offered, and is tasked with advising the government on the minimum remuneration for academic staff in universities differentiated by discipline. Sources of money to the fund will be procured from government allocations, donations, endowments, grants, gifts and other investments.

The Funding Board is expected to reform the system of funding public universities and, in so doing, promote greater transparency with regard to decision-making informing the allocation and distribution of funds to public universities. The Board will also support private universities due to the important role they play in the university system. The rationale for extending public financial support to private universities is informed by the recognition that conditional grants and loans to private universities will not be distributed, or be equivalent to, public funds distributed to public universities. Students in private universities were already eligible to apply for student loans and bursaries through the HELB, prior to the establishment of the Fund and Board. Faculties in private universities, moreover, have access to public research and innovation funds managed on behalf of the government by the Commission for Science, Technology and Innovation. The proposed system of conditional grants and loans to private universities constitutes an important step in the development of a well-balanced university system.

A key challenge to reforming the current system of funding for public universities will be negotiating the practice of levying universally applied fees on government-supported students, regardless of the differentiated unit cost of their academic program. For example, fees levied on a government supported student enrolled in a program in the social sciences, is the same as those levied on a government supported student enrolled in a medical or engineering degree, despite the enormous cost differential implied in delivering these programs. Fees based on differentiated unit costs are being applied in module two for full fee-paying students. The application of differentiated fees in this regard has demonstrated significant utility, and universities have accrued important experience in administering these fees, with the potential to scale up this intervention for application in regular degree programs to regularize fees for all students in public universities. Such a program of action, however, will require a significant awareness campaign targeting the student community and other key stakeholders to promote its rationale and avoid potential confusion. The universal introduction of fees premised on differentiated program unit costs will also need to mitigate the potential for greater inequity in university education.

A second challenge relates to the remuneration of faculty in public universities. Challenges in this regard have already arisen with respect to the payment of faculty who teach module two programs in public universities. There is a need to establish minimum standards of remuneration for academic staff differentiated by discipline. This will regularize the payment structure, and respond to the challenge of staff retention, especially in disciplines that compete with the private sector, such as medicine, engineering and technology.

A third challenge relates to the development of performance-based funding for public universities. Increasingly scarce resources imply ever-more-difficult decisions in the allocation of limited public funds in support of higher education. Historically many governments allocated public funds to universities in proportion to enrollment. This practice had the advantage of demonstrating commitment to the promotion of access to higher education, and ensured a relatively equitable distribution of spending per-student across institutions. However, enrollment is a poor predictor of overall institutional performance. Continued budgetary pressure in combination with rising demand for educated workers, intensifies the imperative for governments to invest in quality university education relevant to the development needs of the country.

Performance-based funding, allocates a portion of a state's higher education budget in accordance with agreed upon performance criteria. Performance indicators can include, *inter alia*, rates of course completion, measures of credit attainment, graduate output, and equity and gender considerations. This model allows for a more accurate assessment and rewarding of institutional performance relative to national objectives and targets, and can play an important role in incentivizing changes in institutional behavior in support of national development objectives.

Despite the critical role that the Fund/Board is mandated to fulfil in achieving the objectives of wider higher education reform, these institutions have not yet been established by the GOK. The MoEST, however, has indicated that it is initiating interventions to constitute the Fund and Board and that these institutions should be up and running soon.

The Governance and Management of Kenyan Higher Education

The Basis of Autonomy: The Legal Status of Public Universities in Kenya

Kenyan public universities can be described as semi-independent as defined by the relevant statutes. Universities are established as statutory bodies with reasonably clear guidelines pertaining to the roles and powers of key stakeholders. In this respect, the role of the state is largely limited to its role in framing national policies and strategies, with several agencies established to deal with specific regulatory concerns in accordance with clear mandates (for example CUE is responsible for the establishment and accreditation of, and quality assurance as applied to, both public and private universities; KUCCPS is responsible for the placement of government supported students; UFB is responsible for funding universities; and the HELB is responsible for student loan financing).

Upholding the principle of academic freedom is a key driver of reforms introduced and proposed through the Kenya's Universities Act of 2012. Against this background, and in accordance with the "rights-based" Constitution of 2010, it was possible, for the first time, to enshrine the concept of "academic freedom" in law. The Universities Act defines academic freedom as follows:

A University, in performing its functions shall:

a) have the right and responsibility to preserve and promote the traditional principles of academic freedom in the conduct of its internal and external affairs;
b) have power to regulate its affairs in accordance with its independent ethos and traditions and in doing so it shall have regard to:
   i. the promotion and preservation of equality of opportunity and access;
   ii. effective and efficient use of resources; and
   iii. its obligations as to public accountability.

The Universities Act recognizes that universities cannot enjoy unlimited autonomy. Consequently, it introduces several checks and balances to protect the rights of citizens and promote the national interest, and establishes mechanisms through which the government is entitled to monitor and assess institutional performance. Institutions are required to establish governing organs to hold university management accountable for the achievement of institutional goals. Moreover, accreditation and quality assurance systems ensure the quality and relevance of the education and training provided by institutions. Finally, the Act requires that universities adhere to established financial and reporting practices for the purposes of transparency. Each of these limitations on institutional autonomy is discussed below.

Appointment of Leadership to Independent Agencies and Institutions

The process informing the appointment of members of the governing bodies of agencies, and the criteria for their appointment, are guided by principles of competitiveness and transparency. The process commences with a call for applications through advertisements placed in a minimum of two national newspapers. Thereafter a selection panel finalizes shortlisted candidates with the names of both the applicants and shortlisted candidates published in at least two national daily newspapers for public scrutiny. Following the finalization of the shortlist, the Cabinet Secretary responsible for higher education appoints the chairperson and the members of all agency governing organs from the published shortlist.

Criteria guiding the nomination of members to governing bodies are intended to ensure an appropriate mix of competencies, promote gender equity, promote the inclusion of persons with disabilities, and promote participation by marginalized and minority groups. In order that appointed individuals are competent and contribute to the management of university education, the law stipulates minimum educational and experience requirements. A person shall be qualified for appointment as the chairperson of an agency if that person holds a doctoral degree, and has ten years' experience in leadership and management of public or private institutions. At a minimum, other members must hold a master's degree, and demonstrate five years' experience in university leadership, management or academia. In addition to these qualifications, a member appointed to an agency must be a person of high moral character and integrity in accordance with Chapter Six of the Constitution of Kenya.

Following a competitive recruitment process, and on the recommendation of the relevant governing board, the chief executive of each agency is appointed by the Cabinet Secretary, for a term of five years, which may be renewed once. Since the promulgation of the new legislation, the appointment of all chief executives, to the KUCCPS, the TVET Authority, the Commission for Science, Technology, and several public universities, followed these procedures.

Governance and Management in the Public Universities

Prior to the passing of the Universities Act in 2012, all seven public universities were established and accredited by seven contingent Acts of Parliament. Each law was modelled on the law establishing the University of Nairobi, Kenya's first public institution of higher learning.

Prior to 2012, the government maintained close, centralized control on the senior management of universities. The Head of State not only served as the Chancellor of all the public universities, but directly appointed personnel to senior administration and management organs, as well as university officers (members of the Governing Councils, Vice-Chancellors, Deputy Vice Chancellors and Principals of University Colleges and Constituent Colleges).

The Universities Act, 2012, has substantively reformed the administration and governance of public universities. While the government has introduced greater autonomy by withdrawing its constraining system of institutional control, it will continue to monitor the performance of, and play a role in maintaining accountability and transparency within public institutions with regard to their use of public resources. Accountability mechanisms are structured in the form of: a reasonably strong state, and other stakeholder, representation in institutional governance and decision-making bodies, specifically through university councils and the governing boards of other agencies; the introduction of external quality assurance and enhancement mechanisms through the CUE; strengthened internal quality assurance and improvement institutional structures; a strengthened role for the statutory Audit Office with respect to external audit and compliance with financial regulations; and the inclusion of public universities in wider public sector reforms, largely through the introduction of performance contracting, regular audit and increased competition.

New governance structures are being implemented at several levels in the public university subsector: (a) system-wide interventions, (b) institutional interventions; (c) through governing boards, (d) the appointment of senior officers, (e) measures to ensure academic governance, and (f) financial autonomy.

System-wide Governance: Entrepreneurship and adaptability have become part of the fundamental architecture of higher education in Kenya (Kiamba: 2005, a–b). The Kenyan system of higher education has become increasingly complex as it adapts and responds to competition and a rapidly changing environment; increasing demand for quality and relevance; internationalization; and a continuously changing knowledge-led economy. In so doing, the traditional model of concentrated state control has had to be transformed quite quickly towards more sophisticated, flexible, inclusive and responsive forms of governance and management.

Institutional Governance: Senior university officers are usually comprised of the Chancellor (who is the titular head of the institution), the Chairman and Members of the University Council (the governing body of the university), and members of University Management Boards, usually comprised of the Vice-Chancellor as the chief executive, Deputy Vice Chancellors and Principals of Constituent University Colleges and University Campus Colleges. New procedures for the appointment of senior university staff are discussed below.

Appointment of Chancellors in Public Universities: Prior to 2012, Chancellors were appointed directly by the President, without the involvement of the university community. New procedures for the appointment of Chancellors in public institutions require the participation of the university community, in particular the Senate and alumni of the university. The Senate (the primary academic decision-making organ), in consultation with respective alumni associations, identifies persons suitable for appointment. The Senate is tasked with vetting the candidacy of suitable persons, and thereafter forwards five candidates, ranked in order of preference, to the alumni association. The Senate forwards the names of the top three applicants, as ranked by the alumni association, to the Cabinet Secretary for onward transmission to the President, who chooses one person for appointment as Chancellor.

Appointment of Members of University Councils: The process for appointing members to university governing boards (referred to as University Councils) changed substantively with the passing of the Universities Act. Previously appointments were closely controlled by the government. This system has been replaced by mechanisms that blends the appointment of a set of members by virtue of their positions in the government (e.g., Principal Secretaries in the Ministries if Education and Treasury/Finance) with members drawn from the private sector who are appointed through a competitive and transparent process. A Selection Panel appointed by the Cabinet Secretary manages the process of recruitment by advertising vacancies, and the publication of the names of applicants and shortlisted candidates for public scrutiny in at least two national daily newspapers. The Selection Panel then forwards three to the Cabinet Secretary for consideration for appointment to the position of chairman, and an additional nine names for consideration to fill five positions on the relevant boards.

Appointment of the Senior University Management Officers: In 2004 the University of Nairobi, commenced the appointment of senior managers (the Vice Chancellor, the Deputy Vice Chancellors and Principals and Deputy Principal of both Constituent University Colleges and Campus Colleges) through a competitive process. This practice was thereafter adopted by the other public universities. Between 2004 and 2012, however, these processes were not informed by a legal mandate. The Universities Act established a new system to ensure transparency and competition in the appointment of senior university officers. The new system requires the Cabinet Secretary, on the recommendation of University Councils, to appoint these university officers.

Financial Autonomy: Ensuring sufficient and sustainable financial resources is critical for enhancing decision-making autonomy in universities. In this regard, universities in Kenya are permitted to receive funding from donations, student fees (both government sponsored and privately sponsored of full fee-paying students) and to initiate other income generating activities, in addition to receiving funding from government. Income generation on the part of universities in Kenya has injected a new entrepreneurial spirit into the university sector, and enabled universities to assume greater financial autonomy. These imperatives have informed new management structures and behavior more closely aligned with the private sector, through, *inter alia*, the establishment of subsidiary units and companies to manage new sources of finance.[6]

Accountability: Accountability is a necessary complement to autonomy. As governments cede greater autonomy to universities, the need to ensure that institutions remain accountable to approved policies and the use of public resources becomes more challenging. A variety of instruments can be used to offset potential accountability deficits, including, *inter alia*, strategic planning and performance contracting, enforceable stakeholder representation and participation in decision-making processes, financial and academic auditing, and performance monitoring and evaluation. These strategies are briefly examined below.

Strategic Planning and Performance Contracting: The Ministry may monitor a universities' performance against goals set through the signing of annual performance contracts which require institutions to prepare strategic plans, and processes for budgeting and financial audit (discussed below). Strategic planning and performance contracting procedures help to incentivize universities to meet agreed key performance indicators in alignment with national and sector-wide goals, and can assist in promoting efficiency in the use of public funds.

Stakeholder representation: The accountability of universities to various stakeholder groups has been facilitated through the inclusion of representatives of these groups in governing boards.

Financial audit: In Kenya, the introduction of mandatory financial and quality audits are intended to promote transparency with respect to the efficient and effective use of public funds in support of university education, and to ensure that the government and tax base is receiving value in return for their monetary investments. The Universities Act requires universities to prepare annual statements of income and expenditure, which are subject to external audit to ensure their veracity. These statements are subject to the approval of the Cabinet Secretary, and audits reports are forwarded to Parliament for scrutiny by the Auditor General in accordance with Kenyan auditing law.

Academic auditing: With the promulgation of the Universities Act in 2012 academic audits, in support of quality assurance, are initiated under the aegis of the CUE. The Commission has responsibility for establishing educational inputs and learning outcomes for application across all universities in the country.

Performance contracts and competitive funds: The government has devised several mechanisms to steer universities towards contributing to the achievement of policy goals while respecting institutional autonomy, including through the use of annual performance contracts and competitive funds. The introduction of performance contracting is part of a wider public sector reform program which has been implemented over the course of the past seven years. In 2010 the GOK, through the Commission for Science, Technology and Innovation, initiated competitive funding for research and innovation, including the endowing of scholarships and professorial chairs. To intensify the benefits associated with these reforms the GOK should consider the introduction of performance-based funding (including performance-based budgeting) for universities, to be managed by the proposed UFB.

Establishment, Management, Accreditation and Quality Assurance Processes

In addition to the external quality assurance undertaken by the CUE, each university is required to establish systems for internal quality management, assurance and enhancement.

Professional accreditation takes place in parallel to the accreditation and quality assurance processes undertaken by the CUE. This applies to professional degree programs including architecture, medicine, and engineering, and is undertaken by the respective professional associations. In general, professional accreditation is mandated by professional bodies established as professional association or as legal bodies controlled by the professions. Accreditation processes are consequently subject to systems of quality assurance at two levels: institutional and professional accreditation. The two levels of accreditation sometimes operate concurrently or in a consultative manner, but in some cases are implemented completely independent of one another.

CUE largely performs institutional accreditation for all universities. This process commences with the establishment of a university through the granting of a charter, and is subject to regular review of data and reports submitted by the universities, and inspection by CUE for re-accreditation at specified periods. In general, CUE is mandated to ensure that universities comply with criteria in the following areas:

- Admission processes, including the quality and diversity of students admitted to universities;
- The quality of physical infrastructure, including ICT infrastructure;
- Financial management in support of academic programs;
- Information, library holdings and use of ICT in support of teaching and learning;
- Academic programs, and associated internal and external quality assurance mechanisms;

- Governance and management to ensure students, academic and non-academic staff have significant voice in a university's systems of governance and management; and
- Co-curricular services including sports and on- and off-campus learning resources for students.

Kenya has accrued significant experience in administering accreditation and quality assurance in universities through the regulation and oversight of the private university subsector under the now repealed CHE established in 1985. Like all other regulatory bodies, the system of higher education in Kenya utilizes national and international experts to inspect universities and coordinate the peer review academic programs, to improve the quality of private university education and the adoption of modern teaching and learning methods in support of the limited programs offered by private universities. Chartered private universities have adequate learning resources and environment characterized by relatively small classes in the programs that they offer, and a stable and regular academic year predicated on the semester system. A standardized academic year has been less prevalent in public universities and university colleges, which lacked a common year system. On occasion the misalignment of timetables has been heightened by instability caused by strikes. In recent years, however, certainty with regard to the timing and structure of academic activities has improved in the public subsector.

Serious challenges have arisen due to a relatively unregulated public university system which expanded rapidly without due attention to capacity and the resource needs of universities. The public universities have increased revenues through the use of evening and weekend module II (initially called "parallel") degree programs, and through increasing class sizes without an attendant increase in teaching and research capacity, and/or the improved use of modern e-learning teaching methodologies. Furthermore, public universities have established satellite campuses that tend to deliver education of a lower quality than that provided at their main campuses. Public universities have not made significant progress in introducing ICT-led innovations in teaching and learning in response to increasing class sizes. The introduction of external accreditation and quality assurance by the CUE should be considered an initial step towards establishing a new era in the public university sector. It will be imperative to ensure that CUE is empowered with the capacity of required to deliver on a hugely expanded mandate, inclusive of a large and rapidly expanding public subsector.

Diversification of the University System: The Role of Governance in Private Higher Education

The role of the private higher education subsector in expanding access and improving the quality university education delivered will be critical for realizing the GOKs ambitions for the sector. The importance of the private subsector in this regard is premised on the cost implications of expansion, and the limited capacity of the state to support these costs. In many instances existing institutions are unable to respond adequately to the changing needs of the market and private providers have been able to move more quickly to fill gaps in the supply of higher education. In many countries the profit motive informing private institutions leads to concerns on the part of the state that the private subsector may undermine certain values associated with higher education, and the contingent risk that its providers may be unable to deliver quality and relevant education in the absence of a research culture.

Private higher education in Kenya has, however, made a critical contribution to the development of university education in the country. This is demonstrated in table 2.1 which shows that approximately 56 percent of Kenya's universities are located in the private subsector, and that the subsector accounts for approximately 40 percent of total enrollment. The contribution of the private subsector to the country's university sector is, however, quite complex, especially because the number of students in public universities are full fee paying or privately sponsored, presently amounts to about 50 percent of the total student population in public universities (CUE 2013).

Opportunities for learning in Kenyan private universities are limited, with the majority of degree programs offered concentrated in the humanities and social sciences. A minority of private institutions have begun offering degrees in engineering, medicine and other technology-intensive programs. Unlike public institutions, which often duplicate existing degree programs, leading Kenyan private universities make a serious effort to respond to changing market dynamics. Even in the provision of traditional social science programs, some private institutions offer complementary professional courses to improve the market relevance of their degrees. Leading private institutions are also more likely to benefit from strong links to alumni associations and the business community than their counterparts in the public subsector.

The leadership role of private universities is particularly visible with regard to their comparatively more efficient management and planning activities. Compared to public universities, private universities employ smaller staff components, are characterized by more decentralized administrations, have largely succeeded in separating catering from academic services, and employ more efficient strategies for procurement. Inefficiency in the management of private universities may, however, result from the significant influence of religious bodies in some of these institutions.[7] In some of institutions the religious affiliation of employees may surpass their professional competence.

Accreditation and quality assurance regimes in private and public service providers: This policy note has already covered the removal of the dichotomy and the introduction of a level playing field in the establishment and accreditation of, and quality assurance and enhancement measures, between public and the private universities. The entire Kenyan higher education sector is now subject to a uniform regulatory framework under the Universities Act of 2012. In addition to the external quality assurance undertaken by the CUE, each university is required to establish systems to promote the management of internal quality assurance and enhancement systems.

Management systems in private universities: The common regulatory, accreditation and quality assurance systems implemented across public and private universities has led to the adoption of largely similar management systems across the sector. The only substantial difference relates to funding. Whilst public universities continue to receive the majority of their funding from the state, private universities in Kenya are primarily funded by the religious sector; amounting to about 70 percent of all universities. Private universities, incorporate an extra layer of management in addition to University Councils, in the form of a Boards of Trustees, appointed by the university's sponsor. Boards of Trustees, in turn, appoint the Chancellors and University Councils. This large management structures prevalent in the private subsector has led to frictions in the management of universities and may require re-examination as the private university subsector expands and becomes more complex.

Public funding in support of private universities: Private universities in Kenya have received limited financial support from the state. Nevertheless, demand-side financing is used as an argument to support state sponsorship of private higher education. Financing instruments under this category often take the form of "scholarships," "bursaries," and "financial aid." Since 2010, students in private universities, and privately sponsored students in public universities, have been eligible for government support through loans, bursaries and scholarships, which are managed by the HELB.

Staff and faculty in both public and private universities are equally eligible for financial support in form of competitive research and innovation grants awarded by the Commission for Science, Technology and Innovation. These two forms of support, along with other strategies introduced through the Universities Act 2012 (primarily through accreditation and quality assurance processes) contributed to a levelling the playing field for public and private universities.

Learning from Experience

Nigeria offers an example of a higher education system that has had to grapple with similar challenges to those faced by the Kenyan sector. While Nigeria has a much larger population and a greater diversity of institutions than Kenya, there are many similarities between the two countries. Reform in Nigeria followed the passing of the Magna Charta Universitatum (1998) Act which worked to free universities from over-regulation on the part of government; promoted institutional autonomy for public universities; and introduced a number of new accountability measures. Greater institutional autonomy allowed public universities to appoint key officers, determine the conditions of service of their staff, control student admissions and academic curricula, and enabled greater institutional control of finances. This created a foundation in which universities had the freedom to introduce new courses, generate new sources of income, and introduce institutional evaluation and staff appraisals. The federal government, in an effort to further democratize public educational institutions, amended the law in 2003 to strengthen autonomy in the university system. The 2003 Act introduced new mechanisms for public institutions to govern and regulate themselves as independent legal entities without interference from the government and its agencies. Prior to the introduction of these reforms, the President of the country was tasked with appointing and removing the Vice-Chancellors of public institutions. At present, the Council appoints the Vice-Chancellor from a list of three shortlisted candidates. Buffer institutions include the National Universities Commission (NUC), the National Board for Technical Education (NBTE), and the National Commission for Colleges of Education (NCCE).

Evidence suggests that the effect of reform in Nigeria was instrumental in improving governance and operational efficiency. The reforms also helped to reduce the reliance of public universities on the state for funds. There is less agreement on the effect of the reforms on the quality of services provided, and with respect to equity considerations as applied to access and academic success.

Conclusion: Challenges, Opportunities, and Recommendations

Key stakeholders to the rapidly expanding and increasingly complex Kenyan university system will need to address the following challenges to ensure that the country continues to deliver quality higher education in alignment with national development goals:

- *Ensuring the quality of university education delivery in a context of rapid enrollment growth.* Available evidence suggests that the quality of higher education provision in Kenya has suffered due to exponential growth in enrollment which has not been matched by proportional investment in physical and human resources. There is an urgent need to rectify current imbalances, and mitigate imbalance going forward, through improving the remuneration of university faculty and staff; investing in existing and new university infrastructure and facilities; promoting technology in support of teaching and learning; and improving the funding environment for research and innovation. Implementation of interventions in support of these outcomes in conjunction with ongoing governance reforms initiated in 2012 will help to ensure and advance the realization of a higher education sector that delivers quality, relevant and globally competitive education as envisioned in the country's Vision 2030 and the Constitution of 2010.

- *The CUE must be capacitated to enable it to efficiently deliver on its expanded mandate.* The CUE faces significant capacity constraints in fulfilling the responsibilities accorded to it in the management of the private university subsector and the much larger and more complex public university subsector. The CUE will require significant investment and reorganization to effectively deliver on its expanded mandate.

- *Accreditation and quality assurance systems.* The sector has made significant progress in implementing new accreditation and quality assurance systems in alignment with the Universities Act of 2012. However this progress should be reviewed and assessed with a view to accelerating and deepening change. Moreover, the introduction of new structures for accreditation and quality assurance should be benchmarked to international best practices.

- *Steps must be taken to mitigate the potential for conflicts of interest to arise through accreditation and quality assurance processes.* The 2012 Universities Act does not adequately address the potential for conflicts of interest to arise between CUE and relevant professional bodies, with the potential to undermine quality assurance and enhancement processes. The government should facilitate consultation between all key stakeholders to the process, including the government, CUE, professional bodies and universities, with a view to establishing resilient and effective approaches to accreditation and quality assurance.

- *The Universities Fund and Universities Funding Board must be established and capacitated.* Despite the central role accorded to the proposed Universities Fund and Funding Board in realizing the post-2012 higher education reforms, these bodies have not been established. The Board is expected contribute to the introduction of performance-based budgeting and funding to public universities. The potential returns to these and other reforms could be compromised in the absence of timely efforts to establish these important entities.

- *Review the effective functioning and legality of administration and management organs within universities.* Post-2012 appointments of senior management staff, specifically the appointment of Chancellors and University Councils, should be reviewed to ensure that these practices and processes are being undertaken in accordance with the new law.

- *Improving data and information management systems.* There is an urgent need to improve systems for the collection of timely and reliable data to support planning processes and the management of higher education in Kenya. Data collection and information management systems are currently unable to provide quality data with regard to student admissions, academic programs offered, tuition/fees, numbers of staff/faculty, university resources (infrastructure, facilities, equipment, etc.), graduate tracer data, and data regarding employment opportunities. A systemic review is required in support of the establishment a modern information management system. This will be essential to enable CUE and KUCCPS to effectively deliver on their mandates.

- *Improve alternative income generation practices in public universities.* An increasingly constrained public financing environment has led to increasingly entrepreneurial activity on the part of Kenyan universities in support of the generation of alternative sources of income. While the development of alternative channels for income generation should be welcomed, these practices should be reviewed to ensure their continued contribution to the development of university education and to ensure that they are not compromising the quality and relevance of education delivered and/or equity as the system evolves.

Notes

1. The Universities Act, 2012 has defined a "public university" as "a university established and maintained out of public funds" and a "private university" as "a university which is not established or maintained out of public funds".
2. The Technical University of Mombasa and the Pwani University.
3. Garissa University.
4. These were: The University of Nairobi Act, Cap 210; The Kenyatta University Act, Cap 210C; The Moi University Act, Cap 210A; The Jomo Kenyatta University of Agriculture and Technology Act, No. 8 of 1994; The Egerton University Act Cap 214; The Maseno University Act, No. 7 of 2000; and The Masinde Muliro University of Science and Technology Act, 2006.
5. The Universities Act, Cap 210B.
6. The University of Nairobi was the first to do this by establishing the University of Nairobi Enterprises and Services Limited (UNES) in the late 1990s and other universities have followed suit.
7. About 70% of private universities in Kenya have been established by religious organizations.

References

Commission for University Education. 2013. *Needs Assessment for the Expansion of University Education in Kenya 2013–2018*. Nairobi: Commission for University Education Report, by 3D Africa Communications Limited, Commission for University Education.

Kiamba, C. 2005. "Entrepreneurialism and Adaptability in Kenyan Universities in the Face of Declining Donor and Government Support." Paper presented at the Expert Meeting and Conference on "A Changing Landscape: Making Support for Higher Education and Research in Developing Countries More Effective," The Hague, The Netherlands, May 23–25.

———. 2007. *Kenya Vision 2030: A Globally Competitive and Prosperous Kenya*. Nairobi: Ministry of Planning and National Development.

———. 2012a. *Report of the Taskforce on the Alignment of the Higher Education, Science and Technology Sector with the Constitution of Kenya*. Nairobi: Ministry of Higher Education, Science and Technology.

———. 2012b. *The Universities Act, 2012*. Nairobi: The Government Printer.

———. 2012c. *Sessional Paper: A Policy Framework for Education and Training on Reforming Education and Training Sectors in Kenya*. Nairobi: Ministry of Education and Ministry of Higher Education, Science and Technology.

———. 2013a. *The Technical and Vocational Education and Training Act*. Nairobi: The Government Printer.

Environmental Benefits Statement

The World Bank Group is committed to reducing its environmental footprint. In support of this commitment, the Publishing and Knowledge Division leverages electronic publishing options and print-on-demand technology, which is located in regional hubs worldwide. Together, these initiatives enable print runs to be lowered and shipping distances decreased, resulting in reduced paper consumption, chemical use, greenhouse gas emissions, and waste.

The Publishing and Knowledge Division follows the recommended standards for paper use set by the Green Press Initiative. The majority of our books are printed on Forest Stewardship Council (FSC)–certified paper, with nearly all containing 50–100 percent recycled content. The recycled fiber in our book paper is either unbleached or bleached using totally chlorine-free (TCF), processed chlorine-free (PCF), or enhanced elemental chlorine-free (EECF) processes.

More information about the Bank's environmental philosophy can be found at http://www.worldbank.org/corporateresponsibility.

www.ingramcontent.com/pod-product-compliance
Lightning Source LLC
Chambersburg PA
CBHW080742250426
43671CB00038B/2841